Listening C2

Six practice tests for the
Cambridge C2 Proficiency

CPE
C2

Jane Turner

PROSPERITY EDUCATION
www.prosperityeducation.net

Registered offices: Sherlock Close, Cambridge
CB3 0HP, United Kingdom

© Prosperity Education Ltd. 2022

First published 2022

ISBN: 978-1-913825-62-1

This publication is in copyright. Subject to statutory exception
and to the provisions of relevant collective licensing agreements,
no reproduction of any part may take place without the written
permission of Prosperity Education.

'Cambridge C2 Proficiency' and 'CPE' are brands belonging to The Chancellor,
Masters and Scholars of the University of Cambridge and are not
associated with Prosperity Education or its products.

Audio production by FFG Media: www.ffgmedia.co.uk
Actors: Kirsty Gosnay; Rob Holman; Natalie Holman; Sandy Murray;
Tom O'Reilly; Jane Turner; and David and Annie Pickering Pick.

The moral rights of the author have been asserted in accordance with
the Copyright, Designs and Patents Act 1988.

For further information and resources, visit: www.prosperityeducation.net

To infinity and beyond.

Contents

Introduction	2
About the C2 Proficiency Listening exam	3
Test 1	5
Test 2	15
Test 3	25
Test 4	35
Test 5	45
Test 6	55
Answer keys	65
Transcript – Test 1	74
Transcript – Test 2	79
Transcript – Test 3	84
Transcript – Test 4	89
Transcript – Test 5	94
Transcript – Test 6	99
How to download the audio	105

© 2022 Prosperity Education | 'Cambridge C2 Proficiency' and 'CPE' are brands belonging to the Chancellor, Masters and Scholars of the University of Cambridge and are not associated with Prosperity Education or its products.

Introduction

Welcome to this edition of sample tests for the Cambridge C2 Proficiency Listening, which has been written to replicate the Cambridge exam experience and has undergone rigorous expert and peer review. It comprises six C2 Proficiency Listening tests, 180 individual assessments with answer keys and audio transcripts, providing a large bank of high-quality, test-practice material for candidates.

The accompanying audio files to this resource are available to download from the Prosperity Education website (see the end of this book for instructions).

You or your students, if you are a teacher, will hopefully enjoy the wide range of recordings and benefit from the repetitive practice, something that is key to preparing for this part of the C2 Proficiency (CPE) examination.

I hope that you will find this resource a useful study aid, and I wish you all the best in preparing for the exam.

Jane Turner
Cambridge, 2022

Jane Turner is an associate lecturer in EAP/EFL at Anglia Ruskin University, Cambridge, and an EFL materials writer for international exam boards, universities and publishers. She previously worked as a Cambridge ESOL examiner for the British Council, and holds an MA in Educational Management and Cambridge CELTA and DELTA.

About the C2 Proficiency Listening

The Cambridge English C2 Proficiency (CPE) examination is a timed assessment, with approximately 40 minutes assigned to the Listening section, which is worth 20% of the available grade and comprises 30 individual assessments.

The Listening section of the examination tests candidates' abilities to follow a diverse range of spoken English, and to understand the speakers' personal opinions and attitudes, specific information being conveyed and also general meaning of lengthier monologues. It is broken down in to four parts with one mark awarded to each correct answer:

- Part 1 contains three recordings of people speaking in different situations. Each recording is followed by two multiple-choice questions.

- Part 2 is a longer recording of an individual speaking about a specific topic. In each of the eight sentences that follow, a word or short phrase has been removed.

- Part 3 is a longer recording of people speaking about a specific topic. There follows six multiple-choice questions.

- Part 4 contains five short recordings of individuals speaking about a common subject. Each recording is followed by two questions tasks.

In the exam, candidates will hear each recording twice and will be given time to read the questions before the recording is played. In this resource, the recordings play only once.

For more information, visit the Cambridge Assessment English website.

Prosperity Education

Our growing range of tests cover the IELTS Academic and Cambridge English B2 First (previously known as the FCE), C1 Advanced (CAE) and C2 Proficiency (CPE) exam. They are available in print or as pdfs which you can download directly from www.prosperityeducation.net. Each resource has a free sample so that you can evaluate its quality.

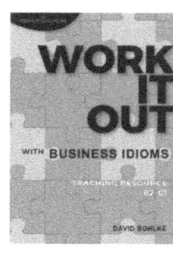

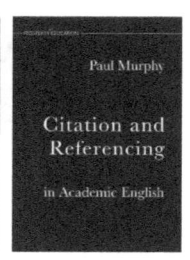

Cambridge C2 Proficiency Listening

Test 1

Part 1

Cambridge C2 Proficiency Listening

Test 1
Audio track: C2_Listening_1_1.mp3

You will hear three different extracts. For questions 1–6, select the best answer A, B or C. There are two questions for each extract. Read the questions carefully before playing the audio. In the exam, you will have the opportunity to listen to each recording twice.

Extract One

1   You hear a woman talking on the radio about a sports event. What is the woman's opinion of the organisation of the event?

   A   The price of tickets was generally reasonable.
   B   The venues were unsuitable for a high-profile event.
   C   The practicalities were well-considered.

2   What does the woman suggest about the event?

   A   There was a lot of controversy about the event.
   B   The event was a failure from a commercial perspective.
   C   The athletes failed to live up to expectations.

Extract Two

3   You hear part of an interview with an educational campaigner, in which public spending is discussed. The campaigner suggests that when formulating policy, the government:

   A   should be more transparent about their decisions.
   B   is reluctant to make unpopular choices.
   C   relies too much on external consultants.

Cambridge C2 Proficiency Listening

4 Which aspect of education does the campaigner feel has been underfunded?

    A Healthy food provision

    B Additional academic support

    C School sports activities

Extract Three

5 You hear a man talking on the radio about a new type of account that has just been introduced at his bank. What does the man say about the account?

    A It offers customers flexibility in their banking options.

    B It encourages customers to monitor their spending habits.

    C It provides cash incentives for customers to save more.

6 The man says his bank makes customers feel that:

    A they are in control.

    B they are individuals.

    C they are valued.

Cambridge C2 Proficiency Listening

Part 2

Test 1
Audio track: C2_Listening_1_2.mp3

You will hear a gem expert talking about a substance called amber. For questions 7–15, complete the sentence with a word or short phrase (a maximum of three words). Read the questions carefully before playing the audio. In the exam, you will have the opportunity to listen to each recording twice.

Amber

Contrary to popular belief, amber is not a **7)**_____, although it is often treated as such.

Resin is a **8)**_____ substance which acts as a safeguard to protect trees from pests.

Amber **9)**_____, such as fossilised leaves or insects, are traces of life that existed millions of years ago.

Most amber **10)**_____ are found in the Baltic region of Northern Europe.

In the Baltic region, there are fears about the environmental impact of any amber extraction that is **11)**_____.

The phrase 'Baltic **12)**_____' has been used to draw parallels between the popularity of amber and nineteenth-century North America.

The high number of amber **13)**_____ on the market reflects the fact that amber is a much-valued commodity.

The succinic acid found in amber has been said to support the **14)**_____, a claim which has been disputed.

Those interested in the spiritual qualities of amber claim that it may improve people's sense of **15)**_____.

Cambridge C2 Proficiency Listening

Part 3　　　　　　　　　　　　　　　　　　　　　　　　　　　　　　　Test 1
　　　　　　　　　　　　　　　　　　　　　　　Audio track: C2_Listening_1_3.mp3

You will hear an interview in which two filmmakers, Tilly Woodford and Lee Davies, are talking about a documentary they have made about animals. For questions 16–20, select the best answer A, B, C or D. Read the questions carefully before playing the audio. In the exam, you will have the opportunity to listen to each recording twice.

16　Tilly says the initial inspiration for the documentary came from:

　　A　experiencing an intense emotional bond with an animal.

　　B　wanting to encourage her own children to appreciate animals.

　　C　realising her understanding of animals was quite limited.

　　D　thinking about her childhood memories of keeping animals.

17　How did Lee originally feel about working on the documentary?

　　A　Curious about whether he would work well with Tilly

　　B　Guilty about having to abandon his other project

　　C　Anxious about working in a different way

　　D　Doubtful about the level of interest in the subject

18　What does Tilly suggest about the man she interviewed?

　　A　He found it hard to take care of his pets.

　　B　He didn't take his pets' needs into consideration.

　　C　He disagreed with Tilly's suggestions about pet nutrition.

　　D　He only focused on the fun sides of pet ownership.

19 What discovery surprised Lee and Tilly most during their research?

    A How far some people go to protect wild animals

    B How little is known about animal communication

    C How much society's attitudes to pets have changed

    D How important the pet sector is to the economy

20 When reflecting on the documentary, they express regrets that:

    A they had to cut several stories from the final version.

    B the documentary contained few of their own insights.

    C they focused on the least controversial issues.

    D their small budget limited what they could do.

Cambridge C2 Proficiency Listening

Part 4

Test 1
Audio track: C2_Listening_1_4.mp3

You will hear five short extracts in which people are talking about their workplaces. Read the questions carefully before playing the audio. In the exam, you will have the opportunity to listen to each recording twice.

Task One

For questions 21–25, select from the list (A–H) what each speaker is primarily responsible for in their job.

Task Two

For questions 26–30, select from the list (A–H) which benefit of working for their company each speaker mentions.

While you listen, you must complete both tasks.

Task One

For questions 21–25, select from the list (A–H) what each speaker is primarily responsible for in their job.

A Formulating marketing strategies

B Approving financial transactions

C Managing professional development

D Resolving customer complaints

E Developing new products

F Analysing sales figures

G Recruiting new staff

H Providing technical support

Speaker 1 ☐ 21

Speaker 2 ☐ 22

Speaker 3 ☐ 23

Speaker 4 ☐ 24

Speaker 5 ☐ 25

Task Two

For questions 26–30, select from the list (A–H) which benefit of working for their company each speaker mentions.

A Flexible work schedules

B A greater understanding of their chosen field

C An enhanced sense of self-confidence

D A highly competitive salary

E Better opportunities for career progression

F Additional work responsibilities

G A supportive work environment

H The chance to work creatively

Speaker 1 ☐ 26

Speaker 2 ☐ 27

Speaker 3 ☐ 28

Speaker 4 ☐ 29

Speaker 5 ☐ 30

Cambridge C2 Proficiency Listening

Test 2

Part 1

Cambridge C2 Proficiency Listening

Test 2
Audio track: C2_Listening_2_1.mp3

You will hear three different extracts. For questions 1–6, select the best answer A, B or C. There are two questions for each extract. Read the questions carefully before playing the audio. In the exam, you will have the opportunity to listen to each recording twice.

Extract One

1   You hear a woman talking about an interior design project. The speaker expresses frustration that the client:

   A   expected too much for their budget.
   B   was unwilling to take design risks.
   C   kept changing their requirements.

2   Which aspect of the final design is the speaker most satisfied with?

   A   The harmony between the various different areas
   B   The clever use of space-saving techniques
   C   The mix of contemporary and traditional styles

Extract Two

3   You hear part of a conversation in which two friends, Tom and Olivia, are discussing university courses. Why is Tom reluctant to apply to university?

   A   He is doubtful about his ability to cope academically at university.
   B   He is unsure that the benefits of a degree outweigh the costs.
   C   He is confused about how to distinguish between similar courses.

4 How does Tom respond to Olivia's point about prestigious universities?

   A He reassures her that universities are changing.

   B He uses employment figures to reject her point.

   C He suggests that she should be less biased.

Extract Three

5 You hear a woman talking on the radio about a company's latest sales figures. The speaker says the sales figures:

   A provide reasons for the company to be cautiously optimistic.

   B show that the profile of company's core consumers has changed.

   C are unlikely to harm the company's long-term prospects.

6 What value does the speaker say the company is associated with?

   A Value for money

   B Quality

   C Innovation

Cambridge C2 Proficiency Listening

Part 2

Test 2
Audio track: C2_Listening_2_2.mp3

You will hear a professor talking about a phenomenon in astronomy called planetary transits. For questions 7–15, complete the sentence with a word or short phrase (a maximum of three words). Read the questions carefully before playing the audio. In the exam, you will have the opportunity to listen to each recording twice.

Transits of Venus

Before Pierre Gassendi in 1631, no astronomer had ever managed to 7)_____ a planetary transit.

Jeremiah Horrocks correctly predicted a transit of Venus after noticing that another scientist's astronomical tables contained 8)_____.

The 9)_____ of Venus transits is due to the planet's complex orbit patterns.

The 1882 Venus transit was described by one academic as a 10)'_____' to witness.

Astronomers used the 11)_____ they measured during planetary transits to calculate astronomical distances.

One unusual observation scientists made during the 1761 Venus transit was a 12)_____ of light.

The 18th-century theory that Venus must have some kind of 13)_____ was later confirmed, highlighting the scientific importance of transits.

The notable similarities and differences between Earth and Venus have led some scientists to refer to Venus as 'Earth's 14)_____'.

Scientists also track changes in the 15)_____ of certain stars during transits to help them identify exoplanets.

Cambridge C2 Proficiency Listening

Part 3

Test 2
Audio track: C2_Listening_2_3.mp3

You will hear part of a discussion in which two economists, Rita Manning and Paul Mason, are discussing the implications of global trade. For questions 16–20, select the best answer A, B, C or D. Read the questions carefully before playing the audio. In the exam, you will have the opportunity to listen to each recording twice.

16   What does Rita say about the fashion industry and globalisation?

　　　A   Most people mainly associate globalisation with clothing.

　　　B   Clothing was the first sector heavily affected by globalisation.

　　　C   Globalisation has made fashion design less creative.

　　　D   Globalisation has raised standards in the fashion industry.

17   What does Paul imply about the concept he calls 'glocalisation'?

　　　A   Big companies get too much praise for adapting to local markets.

　　　B   More legislation is needed to control the actions of big companies.

　　　C   Consumers benefit from having access to more choices.

　　　D   It's hard to compare local companies and international markets.

18   How did Rita feel when interviewing people for her latest book?

　　　A   Disappointed in consumers' irresponsible actions.

　　　B   Surprised at the factors influencing consumers' decisions.

　　　C   Concerned that consumers' views are being ignored.

　　　D   Hopeful that consumer behaviour is changing.

19 Paul says the greatest impact of globalisation has been the:

   A change in consumers' expectations.
   B increase in multinational corporations.
   C damage caused to the environment.
   D growth of the knowledge economy.

20 Both Rita and Paul express the view that globalisation can help people to:

   A reach new audiences that are interested in their ideas.
   B develop their understanding of unfamiliar cultures.
   C find solutions to the world's most important problems.
   D gain access to better employment opportunities.

Cambridge C2 Proficiency Listening

Part 4

Test 2
Audio track: C2_Listening_2_4.mp3

You will hear five short extracts in which people are talking about living overseas. Read the questions carefully before playing the audio. In the exam, you will have the opportunity to listen to each recording twice.

Task One

For questions 21–25, select from the list (A–H) the main concern each speaker had before moving overseas.

Task Two

For questions 26–30, select from the list (A–H) the main benefit each speaker has gained from moving overseas.

While you listen, you must complete both tasks.

Task One

For questions 21–25, select from the list (A–H) the main concern each speaker had before moving overseas.

A Keeping up with responsibilities in their home country

B Overcoming language barriers

C Adapting to an unfamiliar culture

D Being able to find employment

E Managing their finances effectively

F Dealing with homesickness

G Finding people to socialise with

H Coping with the different climate

Speaker 1 [21]
Speaker 2 [22]
Speaker 3 [23]
Speaker 4 [24]
Speaker 5 [25]

Task Two

For questions 26–30, select from the list (A–H) the main benefit each speaker has gained from moving overseas.

A An appreciation of a different way of life

B Learning to cope with unexpected problems

C Achieving a better work-life balance

D Improving their earning potential

E Introducing a sense of adventure into life

F Discovering a new direction in life

G Learning to be more self-sufficient

H Improving their communication skills

Speaker 1 [26]
Speaker 2 [27]
Speaker 3 [28]
Speaker 4 [29]
Speaker 5 [30]

Cambridge C2 Proficiency Listening

Test 3

Cambridge C2 Proficiency Listening

Part 1

Test 3
Audio track: C2_Listening_3_1.mp3

You will hear three different extracts. For questions 1–6, select the best answer A, B or C. There are two questions for each extract. Read the questions carefully before playing the audio. In the exam, you will have the opportunity to listen to each recording twice.

Extract One

1   You will hear part of a discussion with a high school pupil, in which proposed changes to a school dress code are being discussed. The pupil says the current dress code at her school is:

    A   unnecessary.

    B   restrictive.

    C   confusing.

2   The pupil says that imposing an official school uniform:

    A   establishes equality amongst pupils.

    B   helps to removes pupils' prejudices.

    C   creates a sense of belonging amongst pupils.

Extract Two

3   You hear a woman talking about a community project. The woman is talking to some:

    A   psychologists.

    B   nurses.

    C   police officers.

Cambridge C2 Proficiency Listening

4 What does the woman see as the main priority for the project?

    A Raising awareness

    B Finding financial support

    C Training participants

Extract Three

5 You hear a man talking on the radio about a classic film which has been remade. What aspect of the new version does the man prefer?

    A The choice of lead actor

    B The updated soundtrack

    C The pace of the film

6 What is the man's opinion of the director Nick Alcott's films?

    A They deserve more critical recognition.

    B They appeal to mainstream audiences.

    C They combine tragic and comic elements.

Cambridge C2 Proficiency Listening

Part 2

Test 3
Audio track: C2_Listening_3_2.mp3

You will hear a construction engineer talking about retrofitting, where new sustainable features are added to existing buildings. For questions 7–15, complete the sentence with a word or short phrase (a maximum of three words). Read the questions carefully before playing the audio. In the exam, you will have the opportunity to listen to each recording twice.

Retrofitting

As a minimum, all new construction projects must follow whichever sustainability

7) _____ are in place at the time.

An official award granted by independent authorities is viewed as the

8) _____ of sustainable construction.

The biggest problem with period buildings is that they

9) _____ .

Demolishing period buildings isn't always preferrable, particularly as these buildings are widely admired for their **10)**_____ .

Retrofitting is thought to be an important way to help the country eliminate

11) _____ substantially.

One of the simplest retrofitting techniques is replacing the

12) _____ in old buildings.

The speaker suggests that solar panels used to be too

13) _____ to work well on historical buildings.

Unless engineers have the right skills to take on complex retrofitting projects, they can actually harm buildings by making them **14)**_____ .

Retrofitting should not be viewed as the **15)**_____ in the journey to environmental sustainability in construction.

Cambridge C2 Proficiency Listening

Part 3

Test 3
Audio track: C2_Listening_3_3.mp3

You will hear a part of a radio interview in which two sports journalists, Mike Crosbie and Judy Huntley, are talking about professional sport and the media. For questions 16–20, select the best answer A, B, C or D. Read the questions carefully before playing the audio. In the exam, you will have the opportunity to listen to each recording twice.

16   Mike says his contribution to the *Heroes Awards* will be:

    A   hosting the ceremony.

    B   sitting on the judging panel.

    C   interviewing the winners.

    D   presenting the main award.

17   What is the main purpose of the event?

    A   To put more attention on less popular types of sport

    B   To acknowledge the greatest sporting achievements

    C   To encourage young people to get involved in sport

    D   To celebrate people making important contributions to sport

18   What does Judy suggest about sports journalism?

    A   It is hard to build professional relationships with athletes.

    B   Sports journalism deserves to be taken more seriously.

    C   Sports bodies have too much influence on the media.

    D   There is not enough diversity of voices in the media.

19 What is Judy's main concern about the commercial development of sport?

   A   It is changing athletes' career priorities.

   B   It is taking sport further away from fans.

   C   It is causing problems for poorer sports teams.

   D   It is making sport less enjoyable to watch.

20 When they were writing their book, Mike and Judy had doubts that:

   A   their different writing styles would work well together.

   B   they could offer a new perspective on their subject.

   C   their book would achieve commercial success.

   D   they could find willing interview subjects.

Cambridge C2 Proficiency Listening

Part 4

Test 3

Audio track: C2_Listening_3_4.mp3

You will hear five short extracts in which people are talking about a work-experience placement they did as part of their university course. Read the questions carefully before playing the audio. In the exam, you will have the opportunity to listen to each recording twice.

Task One

For questions 21–25, select from the list (A–H) what each speaker says they did for their work experience placement.

Task Two

For questions 26–30, select from the list (A–H) what each speaker feels about doing work experience as part of their university course.

While you listen, you must complete both tasks.

Task One

For questions 21–25, select from the list (A–H) what each speaker says did for their work experience placement.

A   Worked in a factory

B   Worked for an animal charity

C   Worked for an environmental organisation

D   Worked in finance

E   Worked in a research laboratory

F   Worked in a relative's company

G   Worked with young children

H   Worked in a local clinic

Speaker 1 [21]
Speaker 2 [22]
Speaker 3 [23]
Speaker 4 [24]
Speaker 5 [25]

Task Two

For questions 26–30, select from the list (A–H) what each speaker feels about doing work experience as part of their university course.

A   Impressed by the skills they developed

B   Surprised that it was so challenging

C   Motivated to work harder academically

D   Relieved it was only for one term

E   Frustrated by the type of tasks given

F   Grateful for the support they received

G   Annoyed that it meant less time for their studies

H   Unconvinced about the purpose of the placement

Speaker 1 [26]
Speaker 2 [27]
Speaker 3 [28]
Speaker 4 [29]
Speaker 5 [30]

Cambridge C2 Proficiency Listening

Test 4

Cambridge C2 Proficiency Listening

Part 1

Test 4
Audio track: C2_Listening_4_1.mp3

You will hear three different extracts. For questions 1–6, select the best answer A, B or C. There are two questions for each extract. Read the questions carefully before playing the audio. In the exam, you will have the opportunity to listen to each recording twice.

Extract One

1   You hear part of an interview in which Luca Simonelli, a famous chef, is talking about his career. What regret does the man have about the early part of his career?

    A   Focusing too much on recognition

    B   Being too hard on his staff

    C   Taking on too many projects

2   What does the man say about his travels in India?

    A   They showed him the importance of food traditions.

    B   They inspired his latest business venture.

    C   They made him into a more adventurous chef.

Extract Two

3   You hear part of a conversation between two colleagues about a new company proposal. What is the main objective of the new proposal?

    A   To monitor productivity

    B   To reduce waste

    C   To encourage collaboration

Cambridge C2 Proficiency Listening

4   What is the woman's attitude to the proposal?

    A   She fears it will cause friction at work.

    B   She doubts it will have the intended effect.

    C   She resents having to justify her actions.

Extract Three

5   You hear a woman talking on the radio about her new hobby. She says a common assumption about her hobby is that it is for people who:

    A   intend to perform professionally.

    B   seek the approval of others.

    C   have an extrovert personality type.

6   How does the speaker say she feels when she does her hobby?

    A   Thrilled

    B   Determined

    C   Engrossed

Part 2

Cambridge C2 Proficiency Listening

Test 4
Audio track: C2_Listening_4_2.mp3

You will hear a professor of biology talking about the 'waggle dance', the unique way that honey bees communicate. For questions 7–15, complete the sentence with a word or short phrase (a maximum of three words). Read the questions carefully before playing the audio. In the exam, you will have the opportunity to listen to each recording twice.

How Bees Communicate

The clearly defined hierarchical structure in the colony determines how

7)_____ is divided.

Flower pollen serves as an important source of fat and

8)_____ for bees.

Female honeybees transport pollen back to the colony using the baskets on their 9)_____.

The purpose of the 'waggle dance' is to indicate to other bees in their colony the

10)_____ of flowers.

It is now known that the gestures in bees' waggle dances are not

11)_____ but are actually performed in a systematic way.

The length of the 'waggle run' is thought to represent the

12)_____ to the source.

A 'round dance' is employed when the flower source is

13)_____.

When food sources differ greatly in quality, bees' dance language may be more

14)_____.

According to research, as bee species have evolved, dance language has increased in its 15)_____.

Cambridge C2 Proficiency Listening

Part 3

Test 4

Audio track: C2_Listening_4_3.mp3

You will hear part of a discussion in which two designers, Ed Forbes and Christina Lewis, are discussing the trend of people choosing to live in extremely small homes. For questions 16–20, select the best answer A, B, C or D. Read the questions carefully before playing the audio. In the exam, you will have the opportunity to listen to each recording twice.

16   Christina first realised that living 'tiny homes' had become a trend when:

   A   she saw examples at a trade fair.
   B   she researched them for a TV show.
   C   her client asked her to design one.
   D   her colleagues based businesses around them.

17   Ed says the most important characteristic of a 'tiny home' is that it:

   A   encourages outdoor living.
   B   is easy to transport if required.
   C   uses clever design solutions.
   D   reflects a specific visual style.

18   What mistake did Ed make during his first tiny home project?

   A   Not seeking expert advice
   B   Not researching the legal requirements
   C   Not managing the budget carefully
   D   Not doing more of the work himself

Cambridge C2 Proficiency Listening

19 Why is Christina unconvinced about the tiny homes trend?

   A   There are simpler ways to live sustainably.
   B   The way tiny homes are being marketed is misleading.
   C   People have a natural tendency to want more space.
   D   Tiny homes are less practical than people assume.

20 Ed and Christina say the key to improving the tiny home experience is:

   A   creating more official tiny home communities.
   B   improving the range of tiny home support services.
   C   making tiny home options more affordable.
   D   improving the building quality of tiny homes.

Cambridge C2 Proficiency Listening

Part 4   Test 4

Audio track: C2_Listening_4_4.mp3

You will hear five short extracts in which people are talking about their views on literature. Read the questions carefully before playing the audio. In the exam, you will have the opportunity to listen to each recording twice.

Task One

For questions 21–25, select from the list (A–H) how each speaker feels about literature classes they have taken.

Task Two

For questions 26–30, select from the list (A–H) what each speaker admires most about their favourite author.

While you listen, you must complete both tasks.

Task One

For questions 21–25, select from the list (A–H) how each speaker feels about literature classes they have taken.

A Inspired to broaden their horizons

B Stimulated by the class discussions

C Ashamed by how little they knew

D Thankful it started their love of literature

E Unsure about the long-term benefits

F Discouraged to read classic novels

G Regretful about not taking it seriously

H Disappointed about the narrow scope

Speaker 1 [21]
Speaker 2 [22]
Speaker 3 [23]
Speaker 4 [24]
Speaker 5 [25]

Task Two

For questions 26–30, select from the list (A–H) what each speaker admires most about their favourite author.

A Their unpredictable plot twists

B The complexity of their characters

C The moral dilemmas they discuss in their work

D The dark humour of their novels

E Their natural use of language

F The wide range of themes they cover

G The descriptions of rural life in their novels

H Their ability to combine styles

Speaker 1 [26]
Speaker 2 [27]
Speaker 3 [28]
Speaker 4 [29]
Speaker 5 [30]

Cambridge C2 Proficiency Listening

Test 5

Cambridge C2 Proficiency Listening

Part 1

Test 5

Audio track: C2_Listening_5_1.mp3

You will hear three different extracts. For questions 1–6, select the best answer A, B or C. There are two questions for each extract. Read the questions carefully before playing the audio. In the exam, you will have the opportunity to listen to each recording twice.

Extract One

1   You hear part of an interview with Ronnie Wilkes, the coach of a professional football club, in which he is asked about an upcoming tournament. The coach says he sees his club's participation in the tournament as:

    A   a distraction from more important competitions.

    B   a chance to give younger players more experience.

    C   a sign of his club's growing international profile.

2   How does the coach respond to the interviewer's comment about player exhaustion?

    A   He accepts it is an issue, but not as the interviewer suggests.

    B   He argues that this issue affects other teams more.

    C   He suggests a way for the sport to address this issue.

Extract Two

3   You hear a woman talking to some college students about a marine biology field trip. The purpose of the trip is to study:

    A   fish populations.

    B   seawater quality.

    C   beach pollution.

Cambridge C2 Proficiency Listening

4   The woman mentions a previous expedition organised by the college:

   A   to explain what is expected from participants.
   B   to give a warning about some potential hazards.
   C   to emphasise the academic benefits of field research.

Extract Three

5   You hear a man talking on the radio about his work at a bank. The man says the priority for him in his job is to:

   A   promote safe investments to customers.
   B   provide objective advice to bank customers.
   C   assess loan applications from small businesses.

6   What quality does the man value most in business?

   A   Forward-planning
   B   Creativity
   C   Determination

Cambridge C2 Proficiency Listening

Part 2

Test 5
Audio track: C2_Listening_5_2.mp3

You will hear a professor of natural history talking about Lark Quarry, a site of scientific interest in Australia. For questions 7–15, complete the sentence with a word or short phrase (a maximum of three words). Read the questions carefully before playing the audio. In the exam, you will have the opportunity to listen to each recording twice.

Lark Quarry

When tracks were discovered at the site, they were initially assumed to be

7)_____ footprints.

Lark Quarry takes its name from a volunteer who worked on the removal of

8)_____ from the site.

Working with fragile materials such as ancient fossils can be a very

9)_____ task requiring a lot of care.

One of the species noted at the site was a small theropod dinosaur with

10)_____, known as the *Skartopus australis*.

Scientists believe that the *Skartopus australis* lived on a diet of

11)_____ and insects.

The tracks of the 'Winton Foot' dinosaur were found to have more

12)_____ than those of the *Skartopus australis*.

Both the *Skartopus australis* and the 'Winton Foot' dinosaurs would have been

potential **13)**_____ for *Tyrannosauropus*.

The original research team concluded that the dinosaur footprints were evidence

of a mass attempt to **14)**_____ the area.

One rumour was that the original scientific findings were the inspiration for part

of a **15)**_____, although this was later denied.

Cambridge C2 Proficiency Listening

Part 3

Test 5

Audio track: C2_Listening_5_3.mp3

You will hear a discussion in which academics Gordon Mackie and Sophie Blackmore talk about how communication has changed in society. For questions 16–20, select the best answer A, B, C or D. Read the questions carefully before playing the audio. In the exam, you will have the opportunity to listen to each recording twice.

16   In his latest book, Gordon aims to challenge the notion that:

   A   technology has changed the purpose of communication.
   B   linguistic standards in society are falling.
   C   the media influences people's use of language.
   D   the evolution of language is inevitable.

17   Gordon says his main duty as an academic is to:

   A   ensure language traditions survive in modern communication.
   B   record examples of linguistic patterns and trends.
   C   explain the fundamental principles of correct language use.
   D   evaluate different theories about language change.

18   Sophie says the thing she values most in written communication is:

   A   style.
   B   accuracy.
   C   clarity.
   D   tone.

Cambridge C2 Proficiency Listening

19 Why does Sophie use social media posts in her classes?

A To raise awareness of what catches readers' attention

B To show how people alter their communication styles

C To highlight the features of informal communication

D To prove that context changes the meaning of a message

20 What aspect of 'text language' do Sophie and Gordon disagree about?

A Whether it will ever be accepted in education

B Why it may be favoured by young people

C How well it crosses cultural boundaries

D Whether it influences spoken communication

Cambridge C2 Proficiency Listening

Part 4

Test 5
Audio track: C2_Listening_5_4.mp3

You will hear five short extracts in which people are talking about their TV-viewing habits. Read the questions carefully before playing the audio. In the exam, you will have the opportunity to listen to each recording twice.

Task One

For questions 21–25, select from the list (A–H) the type of shows they generally watch.

Task Two

For questions 26–30, select from the list (A–H) what each speaker says they gain from TV.

While you listen, you must complete both tasks.

Task One

For questions 21–25, select from the list (A–H) the type of shows they generally watch.

A Factual documentaries

B Skills competitions

C Sports events

D Continuing drama series

E Quiz shows

F Comedy programmes

G Current affairs programmes

H Travel shows

Speaker 1 [21]

Speaker 2 [22]

Speaker 3 [23]

Speaker 4 [24]

Speaker 5 [25]

Task Two

For questions 26–30, select from the list (A–H) what each speaker says they gain from TV.

A Leisure inspiration

B A chance to be moved emotionally

C Interactive fun

D Pure entertainment

E Different views of the world

F Impressive dramatic performances

G Time to bond with family members

H A chance to escape reality

Speaker 1 [26]

Speaker 2 [27]

Speaker 3 [28]

Speaker 4 [29]

Speaker 5 [30]

Cambridge C2 Proficiency Listening

Test 6

Cambridge C2 Proficiency Listening

Part 1

Test 6
Audio track: C2_Listening_6_1.mp3

You will hear three different extracts. For questions 1–6, select the best answer A, B or C. There are two questions for each extract. Read the questions carefully before playing the audio. In the exam, you will have the opportunity to listen to each recording twice.

Extract One

1   You hear part of a conversation between two colleagues about a marketing campaign they have developed for a client. Why is the client unhappy with the campaign?

   A   It targets the product at the wrong market.
   B   It fails to mention the key features of the product.
   C   It makes false claims about the product.

2   What is the man's attitude towards the proposed changes?

   A   He dismisses the concept but offers an alternative.
   B   He is receptive to combining the original and new concept.
   C   He expresses concerns about whether the changes are feasible.

Extract Two

3   You hear a man talking on a podcast about his favourite piece of music. The man says the music is special because it:

   A   has inspired so many other musicians.
   B   can be appreciated on different levels.
   C   reminds him of an important time in his life.

4   What does the man think the song is about?

   A   Making the most of one's time
   B   Remembering a love affair
   C   Feeling alone in the world

Extract Three

5   You hear a woman talking about a community project being launched in a small fishing village. What is the primary aim of the project?

   A   To preserve local traditions
   B   To promote local tourism
   C   To create local employment

6   What does the woman suggest about the project?

   A   It is under-resourced.
   B   It is well-managed.
   C   It is over-ambitious.

Part 2

Cambridge C2 Proficiency Listening

Test 6
Audio track: C2_Listening_6_2.mp3

You will hear a doctor talking about the health effects of cold water. For questions 7–15, complete the sentence with a word or short phrase (a maximum of three words). Read the questions carefully before playing the audio. In the exam, you will have the opportunity to listen to each recording twice.

Cold Water and Health

In hydrotherapy treatments, the use of warm water is thought to promote 7)_____ in the patient.

Cold water should be viewed as a 8)_____ which can be used to boost people's general wellbeing rather than as a medical treatment.

It's important to remain 9)_____ about some of the bolder claims concerning the benefits of cold water.

Hardening is the process where the nervous system gradually adapts to 10)_____ of stress.

Due to physiological responses to cold water, our 11)_____ may improve after taking a cold shower.

One cognitive benefit of cold water exposure is the impact it has on our ability to 12)_____ for long periods of time.

Blood may circulate at 13)_____ in cool temperatures, which may be beneficial for our physical health.

An increase in the number of 14)_____ is believed to have a positive effect on our immune system.

It is recommended that people adjust to cold water exposure 15)_____ rather than attempting to make drastic changes.

Cambridge C2 Proficiency Listening

Part 3

Test 6
Audio track: C2_Listening_6_3.mp3

You will hear part of a discussion in which two business owners, Anya Stern and Vincent Chambers, are talking about their experiences of launching their own businesses. For questions 16–20, select the best answer A, B, C or D. Read the questions carefully before playing the audio. In the exam, you will have the opportunity to listen to each recording twice.

16 Anya says she realised at an early age that:

   A comparing yourself with others is a mistake.
   B the difference between success and failure can be small.
   C hard work is no guarantee of success.
   D staying at the top is harder than reaching it.

17 Why was Vince initially reluctant to start his own business?

   A He didn't want to sacrifice his corporate career.
   B He didn't want to take any financial risks.
   C He didn't see himself as a typical business leader.
   D He didn't think he had enough knowledge.

18 How does Anya feel about reality TV shows based on business?

   A Concerned that they put people off from becoming entrepreneurs
   B Angry that they present an inaccurate image of business
   C Confused about who the intended audience is for these shows
   D Disappointed with the narrow scope of these shows

19 Anya and Vince both say they started their business ventures:

　　A as a way to take control of their life.
　　B at the right time in their life.
　　C with a clear idea of their strategy.
　　D with a desire to change their industries.

20 Vince says the most important quality for a business owner is:

　　A the ability to stay calm under pressure.
　　B the ability to adapt to unforeseen circumstances.
　　C the vision to do things differently.
　　D the courage to ignore critics.

Cambridge C2 Proficiency Listening

Part 4

Test 6
Audio track: C2_Listening_6_4.mp3

You will hear five short extracts in which people are talking about their decision to pursue postgraduate study – the higher studies some people do after completing their undergraduate degree. Read the questions carefully before playing the audio. In the exam, you will have the opportunity to listen to each recording twice.

Task One

For questions 21–25, select from the list (A–H) the main challenge each speaker has faced during their postgraduate study.

Task Two

For questions 26–30, select from the list (A–H) how each speaker feels about their university experience.

While you listen, you must complete both tasks.

Task One

For questions 21–25, select from the list (A–H) the main challenge each speaker has faced during their postgraduate study.

A Dealing with the change to their financial stability

B Meeting the high academic standards

C Adapting to more independent mode of study

D Completing unfamiliar types of tasks

E Making original contributions to their field

F Managing work and academic commitments

G Analysing subjects in such depth

H Knowing how to respond to tutors' feedback

Speaker 1 [21]
Speaker 2 [22]
Speaker 3 [23]
Speaker 4 [24]
Speaker 5 [25]

Task Two

For questions 26–30, select from the list (A–H) how each speaker feels about their university experience.

A Surprised that postgraduate study is so lonely

B Satisfied with what they have achieved

C Frustrated that they have lost interest in their subject

D Motivated to pursue an academic career

E Reassured by their enhanced career prospects

F Concerned that they are unsuited to postgraduate study

G Grateful for the chance to work at their own pace

H Confident that they have chosen the right field

Speaker 1 [26]
Speaker 2 [27]
Speaker 3 [28]
Speaker 4 [29]
Speaker 5 [30]

Cambridge
C2 Proficiency
Listening

Answers

Cambridge C2 Proficiency Listening

Test 1

Part 1							
1	C	2	A	3	B	4	A
5	B	6	C				

Part 2	
7	precious stone
8	sticky
9	inclusions
10	deposits
11	unregulated
12	gold rush
13	imitations
14	immune system
15	intuition

Part 3					
16	B	17	D	18	B
19	C	20	A		

Part 4					
21	C	22	H	23	F
24	D	25	A	26	B
27	E	28	G	29	A
30	C				

Answers

Test 2

Part 1

1	C	2	A	3	B	4	A
5	C	6	B				

Part 2

7	record
8	errors / mathematical errors
9	rarity
10	delight
11	angles
12	ring
13	atmosphere
14	evil twin
15	brightness

Part 3

16	B	17	A	18	D
19	D	20	C		

Part 4

21	B	22	F	23	D
24	A	25	E	26	G
27	C	28	H	29	F
30	B				

Cambridge C2 Proficiency Listening

Test 3

Part 1

1	C	2	C	3	B	4	A
5	A	6	B				

Part 2

7	regulations
8	gold standard
9	waste energy
10	charm / visual charm
11	carbon emissions
12	light bulbs
13	large
14	damp
15	silver bullet

Part 3

16	A	17	D	18	C
19	B	20	B		

Part 4

21	A	22	H	23	E
24	B	25	G	26	D
27	C	28	F	29	E
30	B				

Answers

Test 4

Part 1

1	A	2	C	3	B	4	C
5	C	6	A				

Part 2

7	labor / labour
8	protein
9	legs / rear legs
10	location
11	random
12	distance
13	nearby
14	effective
15	complexity

Part 3

16	D	17	C	18	B
19	D	20	A		

Part 4

21	H	22	C	23	F
24	B	25	A	26	D
27	G	28	C	29	A
30	E				

Cambridge C2 Proficiency Listening

Test 5

Part 1

1	B	2	A	3	A	4	C
5	B	6	A				

Part 2

7	bird
8	rock
9	delicate
10	three toes
11	small mammals / mammals
12	variation
13	prey
14	flee
15	film

Part 3

16	B	17	B	18	C
19	D	20	A		

Part 4

21	F	22	B	23	D
24	E	25	A	26	G
27	A	28	H	29	C
30	E				

Answers

Test 6

Part 1

| 1 | C | 2 | B | 3 | B | 4 | A |
| 5 | A | 6 | C | | | | |

Part 2

7	relaxation
8	tool / simple tool
9	dubious
10	moderate levels
11	mood
12	concentrate
13	faster rates
14	white blood cells
15	gradually

Part 3

| 16 | C | 17 | C | 18 | A |
| 19 | D | 20 | B | | |

Part 4

21	C	22	F	23	G
24	A	25	E	26	B
27	H	28	D	29	C
30	E				

PROSPERITY EDUCATION
www.prosperityeducation.net

Cambridge C2 Proficiency Listening

Transcripts

Cambridge C2 Proficiency Listening

Test 1

Part 1

Audio track: C2_Listening_1_1.mp3

Part 1. You will hear three different extracts. For questions 1 to 6, you must choose the best answer: A, B or C. There are two questions for each extract.

Extract 1 **You hear a woman talking on the radio about a sports event. Now look at questions 1 and 2.**

After three weeks of open-air swimming, track and field, rowing and triathlon events, the Student Outdoor Games have drawn to a close. And what a slick operation it was this year! The organisers covered all bases to ensure the events ran smoothly for competitors and spectators alike. They had even accounted for our notoriously unpredictable weather with new state-of-the-art stadia with retractable roofs. This kept the disruption caused by sudden downpours to a minimum! Visitors could also enjoy improved transport infrastructure, accommodation and hospitality offerings. However, such investments aren't cheap, which may explain the sharp rise in ticket prices this year. But in any case, with the high-profile corporate sponsorship deals and excellent TV ratings, the accountants will be delighted with the revenue generated.

As for the event itself, there's no doubt we witnessed many of the outstanding athletic performances we'd been promised. But as brightly as the athletes shone, their efforts were somewhat eclipsed by the negative publicity caused by multiple allegations of bribery and cheating. Sadly, these scandals hung over the Games, threatening the event's wholesome reputation as a symbol of fair play and team spirit. Let's hope lessons will be learnt before the next Games.

Extract 2 **You hear part of an interview with an educational campaigner, in which public spending is discussed. Now look at questions 3 and 4.**

Speaker 1 Governments have to make difficult decisions about how to allocate resources. So, which factors should the government be considering when developing policies?

Speaker 2 Well, I take your point about budgetary constraints. That's precisely why leaders have to seek unbiased advice from independent subject experts. My concern is that too often, the temptation is to focus more on what will play well in opinion polls. But often, the most beneficial course of action isn't necessarily the one that will win votes. I'm not saying the government has to announce the rationale for every single decision it takes, providing they are basing their policies on sound, logical principles.

Speaker 1 So, you're dissatisfied with the direction the government has been taking?

Speaker 2 Look, I certainly applaud the government's efforts to invest in more tuition and coaching for pupils who are struggling. And for moving physical education higher up the agenda. This commitment to fitness is commendable. But unless the government addresses the question of access to proper nutrition, we can't maximise the benefits of the other initiatives. Many schools simply cannot afford to offer well-balanced meals. Government spending in this area has to be increased significantly because it's been neglected for far too long.

Transcripts

Extract 3   **You hear a man talking on the radio about a new type of account that has just been introduced at his bank. Now look at questions 5 and 6.**

Not so long ago, there wasn't much to distinguish one bank account from another. But that seems to be changing now, with banks offering all sorts of financial bonuses and other perks to lure new customers away from their competitors. And banks are also responding to people's changing lifestyles, as underlined by the growing popularity of mobile and online banking. And my bank has just launched an account which offers regular insights and suggestions about customers' transactions. It's not a savings account, but by making it easier for customers to analyse their expenditure, it does help people to make smarter financial choices. And who doesn't want to get to grips with their finances and manage things better? It also highlights that a 'one-size-fits-all' approach no longer works in banking. Instead, my bank is catering their support to meet customers' unique circumstances. As a result, customers are left feeling confident that they are important to the bank. And the fact that my bank gets such consistently high customer ratings proves that it's a smart move.

Part 2

Audio track: C2_Listening_1_2.mp3

Part 2. You hear a gem expert talking about a substance called amber. For questions 7 to 15, complete the sentences with a word or short phrase.

Today's talk is about something that you'll no doubt have seen in jewellery and decorative objects, and that is amber. This fascinating substance varies in hue from white and grey to the more familiar yellow-brown tones.

And I use the term 'substance' advisedly. Amber is a wood resin, a fact that's perhaps hard to reconcile with its brilliant, shiny appearance! And of course, to all intents and purposes, it's used in jewellery production in much the same way as diamonds, pearls or any other precious stone are used.

But yes, strictly speaking, amber is essentially the resin of ancient trees. Now, many trees produce resin. Resin acts as a form of protection for the trees against disease and pests. In its original form, resin is sticky, almost like glue. When resin drops to the ground, it may lie undisturbed for millennia, and will eventually harden to form amber.

You may have seen some examples of amber containing fossilised plant matter like leaves, or even reptiles and insects. These are called 'inclusions', and it's incredible to think that they're millions of years old.

In terms of geographical distribution, amber is found in a wide range of places, including such diverse regions as the Caribbean and Southeast Asia. However, Northern Europe is the predominant source of amber, with more deposits found in the Baltic region than anywhere else in the world.

Indeed, the amber trade in the Baltic region is so lucrative that it's led to a surge in amber mining in recent years, though not necessarily in compliance with the official procedures. This is causing considerable concern amongst environmentalists. They rightly highlight how unregulated amber extraction in particular degrades the environment, leading to barren landscapes and polluted waterways.

Much to environmentalists' dismay, the market for amber shows no signs of abating. As long as amber remains a highly valued commodity, it will attract unscrupulous individuals willing to exploit natural resources for a quick profit. In fact, the term 'Baltic gold rush' has been coined to describe how the frenzy for amber is affecting the local area – a clear allusion to the impact of the discovery of large amounts of precious metal in nineteenth-century California.

The commercial price of amber varies depending not only on the size of the piece, but other factors such as its purity, colour and shape. Unfortunately, the fact that amber is so highly valued has led to many imitations flooding the market, things that could be made from coloured glass, plastic or many other materials.

Of course, this begs the question: why is there such demand for amber? It's unquestionably attractive, which is why it's primarily used to make visually striking objects and wearable pieces. However, it's also prized for its supposed medicinal qualities, and has been for millennia. For instance, physicians in Ancient Rome used amber to treat conditions affecting the stomach, eyes and throat. And traditional Chinese medicine continues to make use of amber in some treatments. It's also been proposed that the succinic acid found in amber can alleviate pain and strengthen the immune system, although such claims are controversial.

And putting aside the scientific merits of any claims about how amber can benefit our physical health, many people are convinced that amber has spiritual properties. Those who believe in such things insist that it can clear the environment from so-called negative energy, and even enhance a person's intuition. Now, such beliefs are far beyond my scope as an expert in the production and trade of gems and minerals! However, they do underline the fact that humans' love affair with this mysterious resin endures.

Part 3

Audio track: C2_Listening_1_3.mp3

Part 3. You hear an interview in which two filmmakers, Tilly Woodford and Lee Davies, are talking about a documentary they have made about animals. For questions 16 to 20, choose the best answer: A, B, C or D.

Interviewer	Our guests today are the acclaimed filmmakers Tilly Woodford and Lee Davies, who for their latest work have swapped film stars for a four-legged cast! Lee, can you tell us more?
Speaker 1	Well, it's basically about the relationship between people and their pets, and well, animals in general. I'll let Tilly explain as it was originally her idea.
Speaker 2	Yes, growing up on a farm, my parents taught me at an early age all about the practical side of having working animals. But I had an entirely different relationship with the domestic animals we kept as pets. I didn't really question that until I had children of my own. I was determined to raise them to be animal lovers, and that was really the starting point of the documentary. Lee and I started collecting these incredible stories of people whose lives had been transformed in some way by pets. It's taught us a lot about why people can have such strong attachment to their pets.
Speaker 1	We must've spent at least two years doing the research. That first year was particularly hard because I was trying to juggle other work commitments too, do you remember? I felt really bad because Tilly ended up doing far more work than me! To be honest, I was somewhat sceptical at the start that enough people would want to watch a documentary about this particular topic. But I trusted Tilly. Our previous collaborations had been so rewarding. And of course, as a creator, it's always a privilege to take on a new challenge.
Speaker 2	Well, you soon saw the potential once we got underway.
Speaker 1	Definitely! We uncovered so many touching stories.
Speaker 2	Yes, and I know that documentary makers have to be impartial observers. But that wasn't easy for me as someone who cares deeply about animal welfare. What about that YouTuber we interviewed? He was basically exploiting his pets to attract more followers. He was dressing them up in stupid outfits and filming them. But off-camera, he had no interest in those poor pets. And he seemed to find it funny to feed them things they really shouldn't be consuming. It was really hard not to intervene.
Speaker 1	I hasten to add that this was the exception! It was reassuring to spend time with so many responsible pet owners. Had it not been for meeting all those people, I don't think I would've realised how pet-friendly we've become as a nation. And it was also

Transcripts

heartening to learn about all the fantastic animal-conservation work people are doing. It's so important.

Speaker 2 We've absolutely become a society that values our pets. This hadn't occurred to me either until we started making this documentary. I suppose the booming pet-care sector is the logical extension of that change. Personally, my highlight during our research was meeting animal-behaviour experts deciphering what pets might be trying to tell us. Absolutely fascinating!

Speaker 1 At the risk of showing off, I'd say the documentary covers all these issues well. When you're dealing with individuals' personal experiences, it can easily become far too sentimental. Balancing it with factual content is important, especially subjects that provoke debate. Considering we had such tight financial constraints, I'm incredibly proud of what we achieved. I just wish we could have kept in all the content we originally filmed, but it just wasn't feasible.

Speaker 2 Well, I'm just glad we didn't let our personal views or prejudices influence the documentary too much. That would have been a mistake. But like you say, I'll always wonder whether we should have kept in some of the parts we removed. I suspect all documentary makers hate the editing process!

Interviewer Lee, Tilly, thanks…

Part 4

Audio track: C2_Listening_1_4.mp3

Part 4. You hear five short extracts in which people are talking about their workplaces. For questions 21 to 30, choose from the list A–H.

Extract 1

Working in retail isn't what I'd envisaged when I graduated, so it's quite amusing that I work for a major supermarket. But actually, my specific role is in precisely my area of expertise. I'm the person who organises staff workshops and courses. Professional training like this enables employees to enhance their skills in certain areas, be it communication, leadership or specific role-related things like using a particular piece of software. What I love about my job is that I'm building on my existing knowledge of approaches to staff training. It's very motivating.

Extract 2

I'd be lying if I said I wanted to be in the same role that I'm doing now in three years' time. Not that I'm unhappy particularly, but I've always been very ambitious. Having the chance to climb the career ladder is important to me, and that's why I decided to work for the company I'm with now. They offer fantastic routes into management. I'm in the IT department, helping colleagues when they're struggling with the technology. It's a role I enjoy, but I'd like to have a bigger say in the systems and equipment we use. I wouldn't mind a raise, either!

Cambridge C2 Proficiency Listening

Extract 3

Prior to this job, I'd always been in public-facing positions, like dealing with customers who were unhappy with a product. But my current role is about evaluating how the company's doing and deciding how we can improve. My main duty is to look at how we're performing in different markets, in terms of how much we're selling, and where. The work's very interesting and suits my statistical skills. But I wouldn't have settled in so quickly had it not been for the friendly team I'm working with. There's always someone ready to lend a hand if you need help.

Extract 4

I'm in a role where I often have to deal with negative situations, so communication skills are key. And it might sound like a cliché, but I do feel like I make a difference in my job. I get great satisfaction from fixing people's problems. When the customer puts the phone down, they're happier than when they started the call. The pay's nothing special, but what I appreciate about my job is being able to choose the hours I work. Provided I meet the targets the company sets, I can start and finish when I want.

Extract 5

Do I work for a big company? Put it this way: go anywhere in the world and you'll instantly see someone wearing our trainers or a T-shirt with our logo! I'm responsible for planning how we can generate interest in our new range and promote our brand. It's an exciting role because trends are constantly evolving. At first, I wasn't sure that I'd succeed when my manager asked me to take the role on. But seeing how well I've adapted proves that I'm capable of far more than I'd imagined. It's so empowering to know your colleagues trust your judgement.

Transcripts

Test 2

Part 1

Audio track: C2_Listening_2_1.mp3

Part 1. You will hear three different extracts. For questions 1 to 6, you must choose the best answer: A, B or C. There are two questions for each extract.

Extract 1 **You hear a man talking about an interior design project. Now look at questions 1 and 2.**

Many interior design trainees assume they'd never sacrifice their aesthetic principles. But in the real world, compromise is key! Take my last commission. The brief was to transform the traditional living and dining rooms of a home into an open-plan space more in keeping with modern family living. At the initial consultation, the client was keen to do something bold, and was clear about what they were prepared to spend. I wasn't completely on board with the colours they'd insisted on using, but I tailored my scheme accordingly. No sooner had the decorators started putting paint on the walls than the client decided they wanted a more understated look. I'd tried to steer them towards that in the first place! If they'd listened, they'd have saved a lot of time and money. In fact, throughout the entire project, the client constantly moved the goalposts. But as annoying as that was, they were delighted with the end result. Their favourite part was that I'd maximised the space through smart storage solutions. They were also happy I'd retained the space's original seventeenth-century features. I'm especially proud of how the space flows – the dining, relaxing and studying zones are distinct, but are still tied together visually.

Extract 2 **You hear part of a conversation in which two friends, Tom and Olivia, are discussing university courses. Now look at questions 3 and 4.**

Speaker 1 You really should get your application sorted, Tom. The deadlines are looming. Don't leave it to the last minute to apply to the best universities.

Speaker 2 I haven't decided if I'll bother at all.

Speaker 1 Whyever not? You're the brightest student in our class – you'd have the pick of places, and sail through your degree!

Speaker 2 Olivia, I'm sure I'd do well at university, and it might be useful. But once you factor in the tuition costs, the three-year commitment, and all the other expenses on top, it doesn't strike me as a good deal. I've sifted through the hundreds of business courses, and they're all virtually the same. I'd rather learn on the job instead.

Speaker 1 But imagine what a degree from a top-notch university would do for your career prospects. The rest of us graduating from second-rate places will have to try twice as hard to stand out, you know!

Speaker 2 The so-called prestigious institutions play on this outdated idea to lure more students in, thereby reinforcing the myth! But the gap between universities has narrowed a lot. It isn't the gulf you fear, so I wouldn't worry. Statistically speaking, I'd be astonished if where you graduate from affects your chances of finding work.

Speaker 1 But that's not the point I'm making…

Cambridge C2 Proficiency Listening

Extract 3 **You hear a woman talking on the radio about a company's latest sales figures. Now look at questions 5 and 6.**

Speaker 1 And here's our business correspondent, Lucy Harris, with some news about one of the most recognisable brands on our high street.

Speaker 2 Thanks Ed. Yes, the latest sales figures from fashion retailer Blue Ocean are uncomfortable news for shareholders. There's been a notable slump in leisurewear sales, an area where the company traditionally performs well. It's too early to tell whether this is a sign the company's no longer meeting customers' needs, or perhaps evidence of a wider issue in retail. But in light of Blue Ocean's recent acquisition of its main competitor, *Stokes*, the retailer looks set to bounce back from these disappointing sales. As you said, it's an extremely well-known brand. But let's face it, Blue Ocean wouldn't be the first name to come to mind if we're thinking of cutting-edge fashion. So, will these figures highlight the need to move towards the cheaper end of the market in the hope of attracting a younger clientele? And if so, will they abandon the classic, well-made ranges that have made them so popular for decades? Time will tell, Ed.

Part 2

Audio track: C2_Listening_2_2.mp3

Part 2. You hear a professor talking about a phenomenon in astronomy called planetary transits. For questions 7 to 15, complete the sentences with a word or short phrase.

Today's talk is about planetary transits. So, let's start with some key terminology. The Celestial bodies in our Solar System revolve around the parent star, the Sun, a movement called an orbit. When a smaller planet passes between an observer and the much larger Sun, its form can be seen reflected against the face of the Sun. This is called a transit. From Earth, only the planets Mercury and Venus can be seen to pass in front of the Sun.

This phenomenon has been documented by astronomers since the seventeenth century. French astronomer Pierre Gassendi became the first astronomer in history to record a planetary transit. His data on a Mercury transit in 1631 enabled fellow scientists to make crucial astronomical calculations.

Subsequently, the German scientist Johannes Kepler calculated that Venus would pass close to the Sun, but not in front of it. However, the English astronomer Jeremiah Horrocks noticed some mathematical errors in Kepler's astronomical tables, and realised there would be an actual transit of Venus. His prediction was correct, and in 1639 Horrocks became the first person to witness a Venus transit.

What Horrocks managed to do was an important feat itself given the rarity of Venus transits. Venus transits are known to occur in pairs, with the second appearing eight years after the first. The next set of transits will occur around 120 years later. With such complex orbit patterns, relatively few people have a chance to witness one in their lifetime.

And it should also be noted that predicting their occurrence is one thing, but sightings are another thing altogether. Some Venus transits can only be seen from certain parts of the world, if at all. One professor, Sir Robert Ball, wrote that witnessing a Venus transit in 1882 brought "more delight than can easily be expressed".

Poetic descriptions aside, transits are also a vital source of scientific information. For instance, long before the invention of sophisticated radar technology, transits helped astronomers make estimations about the distance between the Sun and the Earth, and the size of the Solar System. In simple terms, their calculations were based on measuring the angle between the visible planet and the Sun.

Planetary transits usually resemble a dark spot against the Sun's solar disc. However,

Transcripts

the 1761 transit of Venus alerted scientists to something strange. They observed a ring of light surrounding Venus, only visible when the planet was near the edge of the Sun. Based on this, scientists drew some remarkably accurate conclusions about the planet.

In particular, what scientists observed during the 1761 transit led them to make an important discovery about Venus. They suggested that Venus must have an atmosphere of some form or another. This was eventually proven to be true. We now know it's dense, consisting primarily of carbon dioxide and clouds of sulfuric acid.

Spurred on by these findings, scientists have continued to uncover the mysteries of Venus. And many researchers now refer to Venus as 'Earth's evil twin'. This evocative term refers to the fact that while the two planets are strikingly similar in size and chemical composition, Venus has a surface temperature exceeding 426° Celsius.

Planetary transits are also used to help scientists learn more about exoplanets, which are planets outside our Solar System. Though these distant planets are too dim to be seen directly, their transits still produce optical changes. For example, when they pass in front of their parent star, it results in a perceptible change in the star's brightness. Tracking such changes can enable scientists to confirm the presence of exoplanets, and even gather evidence of their size and temperature.

Part 3

Audio track: C2_Listening_2_3.mp3

Part 3. You hear part of a discussion in which two economists, Rita Manning and Paul Mason, are discussing the implications of global trade. For questions 16 to 20, choose the best answer: A, B, C or D.

Interviewer Today, we're discussing globalisation and how global trade has affected all our lives, whether for good or for bad. To help us, we're joined by Rita Manning and Paul Mason, two leading experts on economics. Rita, world trade has come a long way, hasn't it?

Speaker 1 It certainly has. We can travel all over the world and expect to see the same brands everywhere. It's something we've grown accustomed to remarkably quickly. Whether that's to be applauded from a cultural-identity perspective is another debate. Obviously, the global clothes trade was an early adopter; that entire industry has been transformed by globalisation. But there are signs of a backlash now. Instant access to cheap, disposable clothes is no longer as desirable as it once was.

Interviewer Most multi-national companies now adapt their goods to cater to individual markets. Does that mean globalisation is changing? Paul, what's your view?

Speaker 2 I think you're referring to a concept called 'glocalisation'. But I'm not sure it's indicative of a change in the underlying forces of globalisation. It certainly doesn't protect local producers, or benefit consumers really. Yes, multinational corporations adapt their goods for different markets, but let's be clear: they don't have noble motives such as respecting local traditions in mind. They're doing it purely because the legislative conditions or consumer market are forcing them to do so. That's why car manufacturers alter their vehicles in accordance with local laws governing things like exhaust emissions. And of course, there are international fast-food chains offering menu options for specific markets.

Speaker 1 But let's not forget consumers have an important role to play in the direction global trade takes. It's never been easier to access the information we need to make ethical shopping decisions. That's something that came through very clearly when I was gathering data about shopping habits for my new book. Having interviewed thousands of people, it's encouraging to see how well-informed consumers are. Yes, they're still motivated by the cost of goods, that's to be expected. But it was a relief to hear them talking about wanting to support local suppliers. And thanks to social media and other means, they're also making their voices heard when they feel multinational

Cambridge C2 Proficiency Listening

corporations aren't acting in society's interests.

Speaker 2 And I'll add that when we refer to globalisation, most people assume we're just talking about the production and distribution of physical products, and how that's influenced our consumer choices. And then from that, media coverage of the negatives of globalisation mainly focuses on issues like pollution and other environmental problems. Rightly so, because we have to scrutinise the actions of huge international companies and what they do in their factories. But we can't have a debate about globalism without acknowledging how it's transformed the market for intellectual capital. I'm talking about things like scientific research, education, IT… the knowledge economy, basically. For me, that, above anything else, has been the legacy of globalisation.

Speaker 1 We can bring in cultural capital as well. Hollywood cinema is one obvious example, or global sports stars. But whether we're talking about coffee, textiles, or indeed ideas, opening up the world as a global market obviously brings benefits. When it's done in the right way, anyway. Let's use globalisation to improve the world by tackling important issues together.

Speaker 2 Yes, provided everyone is given the same platform, I agree. There will always be differences that we'll find hard to reconcile with our own beliefs. Globalisation won't change that. For me, the ideal scenario is globalisation leading to more academic collaboration. We need people from different backgrounds and areas of expertise to work together on the things that affect us all, like injustice, poverty or of course, climate change.

Interviewer Rita, Paul, thank you.

Part 4

Audio track: C2_Listening_2_4.mp3

Part 4. You hear five short extracts in which people are talking about living overseas. For questions 21 to 30, choose from the list A–H.

Extract 1

Living abroad wasn't a burning ambition, but I was offered a huge promotion that entailed me moving to our Tokyo office. All in all, living overseas has been a positive experience. I was worried that my lack of Japanese would hold me back, but I've picked up quite a bit. And as well as all the obvious perks like immersing yourself in a new culture and discovering everything the country has to offer, living abroad has changed me as a person. It's shown me I don't need to rely on other people so much. I've definitely matured, I'd say.

Extract 2

After a lot of discussion, we finally took the plunge and emigrated to New Zealand last year. My husband and I were desperate to leave our stressful jobs, and wanted to raise our children somewhere with plenty of opportunities for outdoor recreation. Of course, I knew there would be times where we'd really miss people back home. And admittedly, I wasn't sure how we'd handle that. But overall, when I compare life now with twelve months ago, I wouldn't go back. We have so much more free time to enjoy together as a family, and a far better quality of life.

Transcripts

Extract 3

My Italian partner and I moved to Rome two years ago. I wasn't worried about settling in, but it did cross my mind that I might struggle to find work. I'd only had a few temporary jobs back in Ireland. It wasn't easy, but I eventually found something, luckily. I'm very happy here. One unexpected reward has been the impact it's had on the way I express myself, even in English. Because I have to concentrate fully to understand Italian, I'm now more alert to body-language cues, and any possible nuances. It's made me more conscious of emphasising my points clearly.

Extract 4

I didn't uproot my life and move to sunny, exotic Brazil on a whim. I'd longed to do it for years, and with the kids all grown up and setting out on their own lives, it felt like the right time. But with all my commitments in the UK, juggling two distinct parts of my life across different time zones was a concern. Fortunately, it hasn't been as hard as I'd feared. And my new life's everything I'd hoped for. I've started volunteering at a local school, which made me realise my future lies in education not banking. I'm so glad I made the move.

Extract 5

Adapting to a new life overseas is anything but straightforward. But that's been the best thing about my move actually. I'm now far better prepared for anything life throws at me: I no longer panic when difficulties arise. I moved to Poland because my grandfather was Polish, and I wanted to explore my heritage. A noble motive, but obviously I had to think about the practicalities. I'd secured a job in Warsaw, but the salary meant I'd have less disposable income in Poland. I was definitely worried about making ends meet on a low wage. But I've made it work somehow!

Cambridge C2 Proficiency Listening

Test 3

Part 1

Audio track: C2_Listening_3_1.mp3

Part 1. You will hear three different extracts. For questions 1 to 6, you must choose the best answer: A, B or C. There are two questions for each extract.

Extract 1 — **You hear part of a discussion with a high school pupil, in which proposed changes to a school dress code are being discussed. Now look at questions 1 and 2.**

Presenter   At present, pupils at Malbridge High School are permitted to wear their own clothes, provided they adhere to the official school colours of navy blue and white. However, plans are afoot to impose a uniform which all pupils will be required to wear. Lucy, as a Malbridge pupil, what's your take?

Pupil   Well... I'm not opposed to the new policy if it adds a bit of clarity. I mean, at present, there seems to be a discrepancy between what lenient teachers think is acceptable for pupils to wear and what stricter teachers will allow. And schools certainly shouldn't let pupils wear whatever we please.

Presenter   So, you wouldn't mind wearing a school uniform?

Pupil   Well, I wouldn't necessarily look forward to it, but I can see the need for it. To be honest, I sometimes feel like school's turning into a bit of a fashion show.

Presenter   So, you think a uniform would make everyone the same?

Pupil   Erm... I don't know about that. Can school uniforms break down social barriers? I think people will still have certain biases or stereotypes, sadly. But for me, I just think if we're all wearing the Malbridge uniform, it'll give us an identity... that we're all representing our school community.

Presenter   Good point...

Extract 2 — **You hear a woman talking about a community project. Now look at questions 3 and 4.**

I'm Dr Maria Knowles, project lead for the Burnford Outreach Association. We help vulnerable residents by offering things like counselling support. The uptake for this service has been tremendous. We've also heard from the authorities that they're intervening in far fewer domestic disputes and disturbances on the street now, something they in part attribute to our work. But we want to go further. Our new project, the drop-in clinic, has the potential to transform people's lives, which is why we're so grateful that you've kindly agreed to volunteer. We have the funding to support ourselves over the long-term, so as we expand you'll be mentoring a new intake of students from the university in order that we can help even more people. But that's for the future. Right now, we need to spread the word so that we reach the people who would benefit from this service. This isn't as easy as it sounds, because many of the people we want to help have, for various complex reasons, slipped through the system. In fact, this is precisely why they have no other way of getting their medical needs met. We need to find the right channels to promote our services so we...

Transcripts

Extract 3   **You hear a man talking on the radio about a classic film which has been remade. Now look at questions 5 and 6.**

Whenever a classic gets a remake, or 'reboot' I think people call it nowadays, there's always the fear that the essence of the film will get lost along the way. But that doesn't mean you need to stick slavishly to the original. Otherwise, what would be the point? I admire this version of *Lydia* because it's retained all the slapstick humour of the original but injected more warmth into proceedings. That's largely due to the inspired casting of Robin Fletcher as Harry. He conveys far more emotional nuance than Walter Peters managed to muster. Admittedly, I didn't recognise the music in this version, but that was to be expected – I dare say I'm not the target viewer! I'm sure younger audiences would appreciate the fact that this version is much zippier than the original, with all the main plot points arising almost immediately. Given *Lydia* is a film that's light on serious drama, Alcott might not have been the obvious choice of director. But then again, if anyone can boost the ratings, he can. There's a reason his films are both lauded by the critics and enjoyed by the public, and that's because of his talent for storytelling.

Part 2

Audio track: C2_Listening_3_2.mp3

Part 2. You hear a construction engineer talking about retrofitting, where new sustainable features are added to existing buildings. For questions 7 to 15, complete the sentences with a word or short phrase.

Today's talk is about sustainability in construction. Now, I know that sustainability is a term that's thrown around so often that people may have lost sight of what it really means. But as construction trainees, it's a key concept which has very real implications for the work you'll be doing.

You're no doubt aware that all buildings are now designed in such a way that they fulfil at least a minimum level of sustainability. To this end, all new buildings must comply with the latest regulations on energy efficiency, building materials and greenhouse gas emissions. These may vary from country to country, and of course many people feel they don't go far enough.

In fact, construction projects which go above and beyond in terms of their commitment to sustainability can apply for certificates awarded by an independent sustainable building organisation. Securing one of these awards is by no means easy, because they're considered to be the gold standard of sustainability.

However, in our country, many people live and work in buildings dating back decades or even centuries. Unfortunately, when they were originally constructed, the concept of sustainability wasn't widely recognised. The main problem with many of these period buildings is that they waste considerable amounts of energy. And that's before we factor in other things like their poor ventilation or sound insulation.

But the solution isn't always to knock them down and construct sustainable replacements instead. In many cases, it simply isn't practical from a financial point of view, especially if it means people having to relocate elsewhere for long periods. And for many people, the visual charm of period buildings makes it unthinkable that they should be replaced with modern alternatives.

That's why retrofitting is becoming increasingly common instead. In its broadest sense, a retrofit is anything we can install into an existing building to improve its green credentials. In fact, many experts point to retrofitting as the key to helping the government achieve its ambitious environmental targets, most notably the vow to eradicate carbon emissions within a generation.

Retrofitting can involve complex or major transformations. For instance, the entire heating system could be changed, as could the flooring, windows or roof. But that's not necessarily the case. For instance, one of the easiest possible retrofits is to swap

Cambridge C2 Proficiency Listening

old-fashioned light bulbs for their modern, energy-efficient counterparts.

Another technique used to improve the energy efficiency of old housing stock is the installation of solar panels. As you know, solar technology has been around for a while. However, there used to be a reluctance to use this on buildings with traditional architecture. Presumably this was because the original panels were so large that they would have looked out of place. However, as the technology has developed, solar panels have decreased in size, making them a more viable option.

As the construction engineers of the future, I urge you to keep up with the latest developments in retrofitting. I'd also warn you that some negligent companies take on retrofitting projects without sufficient expertise. At best, this means the projects do little to make buildings more energy efficient. At worst, it can actually add excess moisture, causing structures to become damp, which as you know will cause a building to rot.

I'd also emphasise that there's a limit to what retrofitting can achieve on its own. It's certainly not a silver bullet that will ensure environmental sustainability. There needs to be a wider debate on the types of building projects we develop in the first place, and where they are located. If we address these issues, we'll be able to maximise the benefits of retrofitting.

Part 3

Audio track: C2_Listening_3_3.mp3

Part 3. You hear a part of a radio interview in which two sports journalists, Mike Crosbie and Judy Huntley, are talking about professional sport and the media. For questions 16 to 20, choose the best answer: A, B, C or D.

Interviewer In today's show, we're talking about sport and media. I'm joined by sports journalists, Mike Crosbie and Judy Huntley, co-authors of the excellent book *Winning Matters*. Mike, you're also involved with the *Heroes Awards*, which will be broadcast live on TV next month.

Speaker 1 Yes. It'll be a novel experience for me. I usually earn my living from behind a computer screen, not appearing onscreen! Of course, standing up and introducing the people giving out the awards is the easy part. I don't envy the committee having to decide between all the amazing individuals, especially for the main category. Really, all those nominated deserve to win.

Interviewer But do we really need another award ceremony for professional athletes? Aren't there enough of those?

Speaker 1 If it were another event focusing on the athletic feats of elite athletes at the very pinnacle of their careers, I'd agree. As accomplished as those individuals are, they already gain plenty of recognition. But the *Heroes Awards* are for incredible performances that just don't get the media's attention. And mainly, the spotlight will be on the unsung heroes of sport. I'm referring to all the people behind the scenes that ensure sports in this country run smoothly. Their role is so vital to sport, and deserves to be honoured. And not just in mainstream disciplines like football. Think about all the people giving up their weekends to organise children's climbing events or to coach youngsters in minority sports like fencing.

Speaker 2 It's a shame the media doesn't cover these stories enough. Actually, sports journalism is at a turning point now, I think. Its profile is higher than it used to be, and most sports journalists are respected now as writers. And the profession's becoming accessible to people from all sorts of backgrounds, which is vital. In fact, that's why athletes are more willing to open up to us now. But here's the issue: is sports journalism as objective and impartial as it used to be? Powerful sports associations are so closely affiliated with media corporations now. So editors put pressure on journalists to change stories that might portray clubs or athletes in a bad light.

Interviewer And we can't ignore how commercialised professional sport has become, especially

Transcripts

the mainstream disciplines, to use Mike's phrase. Should we be concerned about that?

Speaker 2 Well, with the gulf between the top clubs and those with fewer resources, it's hard to make sweeping statements. Are athletes losing their hunger to compete because they're distracted by lucrative advertising deals? It wouldn't appear so, because the standard of sport is rising in our country. But with the vast amounts of finance in sport now, it'd be naïve not to expect changes in the way it's run and marketed. That's my fear. Many people can no longer afford to go and watch live sport or even pay to watch it on TV. Without these loyal supporters, we're losing what makes sport so special.

Interviewer You explored some of these issues in *Winning Matters*. It's your first book together, isn't it?

Speaker 1 That's right. Our different strengths complement one another. But hopefully, the book's very cohesive, rather than two distinct voices vying for attention. We knew there would be great interest in the subject, so we wanted to do it justice.

Speaker 2 Our reputation as journalists gave us access to many people. Everyone agreed to talk to us and put their trust in us, which was great. But we started to wonder whether we were just covering the same topics we'd written about before. We probably both lost some sleep about that, but actually I'm very happy with what we've produced.

Interviewer You should be…

Part 4

Audio track: C2_Listening_3_4.mp3

Part 4. You hear five short extracts in which people are talking about a work-experience placement they did as part of their university course. For questions 21 to 30, choose from the list A–H.

Extract 1

I was so excited about my mechanical engineering placement because it'd always been my ambition to work in the automotive industry. I spent the entire time on the factory floor of a car-manufacturing plant. Observing how engineers resolved mechanical faults was invaluable, and I got great hands-on experience. Well, that's probably the wrong term when talking about heavy, dangerous machinery! But I hadn't anticipated how spending all day in such a noisy environment would affect me. Truthfully, I wasn't sorry when the placement ended. Had it been for more than a term, I might have struggled. I might need to rethink my career plans.

Extract 2

Most medical faculty placements are either in hospitals or local clinics. I ended up at the latter, although I might've had the chance to do a placement at a community organisation, had I requested it. But anyway, the point was to put your theoretical knowledge to the test, and apply it to real-life situations. I loved assisting the staff; the empathy and sensitivity they showed with patients was inspiring. It's underlined that medicine's the right career for me. But it's also highlighted significant gaps in my knowledge. I'm determined to spend more time in the university library from now on.

Cambridge C2 Proficiency Listening

Extract 3

The highlight of my biomedical science degree was the placement I did at the Science Park. It was for a firm conducting trials and studies for the pharmaceutical industry. My classmates did similar placements. It irritated me when they moaned about doing menial tasks that they claimed were beneath them. What did they expect? That they'd enter the lab and instantly find a miracle cure for something? For me, being able to ask questions and gain new insights was brilliant. My mentors were so patient and encouraging, which I really appreciated. They even offered me some paid work over the university holidays!

Extract 4

My degree isn't geared towards a specific career, like nursing or teaching, so I was given a fairly free rein over my work-experience placement. My cousins work in the voluntary sector, which inspired my choice. I selected an organisation that cares for abandoned pets and tries to rehome them. Ultimately, what I gained from the experience was an appreciation of how the voluntary sector operates, like the importance of fundraising. But that's where I could have had an impact during the placement because I had a lot of marketing skills thanks to my business degree. Instead though, they got me doing administrative work, which was a pity.

Extract 5

By the second year of my education degree, I was already sure I didn't want to be a teacher. I'm better suited to academia – researching things like how people learn. But the faculty still insisted I complete a work placement at a kindergarten. I resented having to waste my time on something I had no intention of pursuing later. Even so, I thoroughly enjoyed it. Both the teachers and the kids were receptive to my ideas, which was motivating. However, I wasn't prepared for how demanding it would be. The role requires so much patience, which I'm yet to develop!

Transcripts

Test 4

Part 1

Audio track: C2_Listening_4_1.mp3

Part 1. You will hear three different extracts. For questions 1 to 6, you must choose the best answer: A, B or C. There are two questions for each extract.

Extract 1   **You hear part of an interview in which Luca Simonelli, a famous chef, is talking about his career. Now look at questions 1 and 2.**

I'm one of the nation's so-called elite chefs, but I don't take such accolades seriously. Not now, anyway. If I could travel back in time, I'd tell my former self, the ambitious young chef determined to make it to the top, just to relax a little. Looking back, I can see that this single-minded obsession with achieving critical success and winning awards took its toll. I never had a smile on my face, and I didn't derive any joy from cooking. It's probably why I went from one venture to the next, because nothing was ever good enough for me. I must've been a nightmare to work with! As you mature, your priorities change. I've rediscovered my passion for food, and I've fallen back in love with Mediterranean cuisine. My new restaurant's a tribute to celebrating my culinary heritage. But that doesn't mean staid or boring. In fact, it's been a joy to experiment with new ideas while staying true to my Mediterranean roots. And I think this new open-minded attitude has come about largely through my travels in Asia, and India, especially. Seeing people blending traditional flavours with inventive techniques was a revelation to me and has certainly influenced my new philosophy.

Extract 2   **You hear part of a conversation between two colleagues about a new company proposal. Now look at questions 3 and 4.**

Speaker 1   So, have I understood this correctly? Every single time we plan to be on site we now need to sign in and then out again when we leave?

Speaker 2   That's the plan. Apparently, they're trying to identify the times the building isn't really being used. If they notice regular patterns where we're visiting clients or working remotely, they can adjust the heating or air-conditioning settings accordingly.

Speaker 1   Well, I can see the push to streamline things if the building's empty. The same goes for the lighting as well. But how convenient: they've found a way to keep tabs on us under the guise of helping the environment!

Speaker 2   That's pretty cynical! It might actually be more conducive to teamwork. We may end up making more of an effort to be in the office at the same time as colleagues so that we can catch them in person.

Speaker 1   Mmm. There's that, I suppose. I'm the first person to say we need to find a way to boost team unity and cooperation around here. But I take exception to being spied on. It'll be interesting to see if the move pays off in terms of optimising the facilities.

Extract 3   **You hear a woman talking on the radio about her new hobby. Now look at questions 5 and 6.**

I've recently started doing a few sets at a comedy club, and I love it. Walking onto a stage in front of raucous strangers ready to voice their displeasure if they're not being entertained isn't everyone's idea of fun! And as someone who's somewhat shy in daily life, I don't fulfil the usual stereotype of a standup comedian. But you'd be surprised how many performers are quite introverted in real life. But just to be clear, I've got no aspirations of becoming a star or changing careers. Comedy is just a hobby for me. It's not even about whether the jokes go down well, because applause isn't what I'm craving. Instead, it's about the creative outlet and the feeling I get from overcoming my fears. I imagine it's the same buzz you'd get from extreme sports. But even so, you obviously have to be quite thick-skinned. There's a temptation to give up when you're getting no response from the audience, but you just have to keep going. Another thing I find fascinating is that you can deliver the exact same set of jokes fifty times, but you can never predict which ones will land.

Part 2

Audio track: C2_Listening_4_2.mp3

Part 2. You hear a professor of biology talking about the 'waggle dance', the unique way that honey bees communicate. For questions 7 to 15, complete the sentences with a word or short phrase.

Today we'll explore the fascinating world of one of my favourite insects, the honey bee. We'll focus on the intriguing way these bees communicate, and more specifically, a type of dance they do called the 'waggle dance'. It's called that for good reason, as it involves the bee waggling or shaking their body from side to side.

But as a starting point, note that bees live in complex organisational structures called colonies. There's a clear hierarchy determining the status of individual bees within the colony, and accordingly the division of labour. For instance, some bees will assist with defence, while others are primarily tasked with nest construction, or raising the young in the colony.

And of course, many bees leave the hive in search of flowers that can provide plentiful sources of nectar and pollen for the colony. Nectar is an important energy source for bees since it contains complex sugar carbohydrates, whereas pollen provides them with fats and protein which are vital for their health.

Locating rich food sources is one thing, but bringing food back to the colony is another. Only females can do this as they have a corbicula, or pollen basket, on their rear legs. As the name suggests, pollen baskets enable these bees to collect and transport pollen back to the colony.

However, since honey bees can only transport small quantities each time, it's imperative that they can also convey information to the colony about the location of flowers so that other bees can go out and gather the food as well. And that's actually the communicative function of the waggle dance.

The mechanics of the dance are as follows: the dancing bee first waggles her body from side to side while moving forward in a straight line. Then, she circles back to her starting position, waggles forward once more and again circles back. This circuit is repeated over a hundred times, alternating between clockwise and anti-clockwise directions. To the untrained eye, these movements appear to be random. However, we now know that the bees execute the movements in a specific, systematic way.

Researchers have managed to decipher the meaning of the waggling movement. This is called the 'waggle run', and aims to transmit two crucial pieces of information. Firstly, to communicate the direction of the target, bees plot the waggle run in reference to the angle of the Sun. Secondly, the length of the run is proportionate to the distance to the target. The longer the waggle run, the further away the target.

Honey bees also employ another type of dance, the 'round dance', where the bee simply moves around in a circular motion several times. This appears to be used when the bee is advertising a flower source which is nearby. Researchers have observed that a waggle isn't always included in this dance. When the bee does perform it, the waggle's duration may correlate with the perceived nutritional quality of the flower source.

Following on from this point, researchers in Switzerland have analysed the efficacy of bee communication. Having compared and analysed different types of circumstances in which dance language is used, they concluded that it is most effective when there is great variation in the quality of available food sources.

Now, as an insect expert, I may be biased, but to me, bees' dance language is remarkably sophisticated in terms of the information it can communicate with such a limited range of gestures. In fact, the complexity of this language system has actually evolved over time. Studies have shown, for instance, that older bee species use a simpler form of dance language.

Part 3

Audio track: C2_Listening_4_3.mp3

Part 3. You hear part of a discussion in which two designers, Ed Forbes and Christina Lewis, are discussing the trend of people choosing to live in extremely small homes. For questions 16 to 20, choose the best answer: A, B, C or D.

Interviewer   Today we're discussing so-called 'tiny homes' with interior designers Ed Forbes and Christina Lewis, hosts of the show *Homes with Heart*. Christina, it feels like the tiny homes trend has exploded in recent years.

Speaker 1   Yes, even though actually, the early models, basically pre-constructed wooden cabins, have been around for years. I remember seeing them at trade fairs. But it wasn't something any of my clients would ever have wanted. A story about tiny homes would occasionally feature on one of my programmes, but they were still seen as something eccentric. All that's changed now. Interior design professionals, people I've worked with for years, have even set up consultancies specialising in tiny homes. That's when it became clear to me that tiny homes had crossed over to the mainstream.

Speaker 2   And in *Homes with Heart*, the producers wanted us to explain the concept to people that may be confused about the term.

Interviewer   You've just pre-empted my next question! What exactly are tiny homes?

Speaker 2   Well, some people insist tiny homes must be under 120 square meters, but I think it's more important to understand the underlying principles. It's all about applying smart design principles to maximise space and avoid waste. The vital thing is that everything's intended to serve a particular purpose. But you don't have to sacrifice style to achieve this. Many tiny homes look stunning, especially the ones that take inspiration from natural, rural environments. And many of them come with wheels so they're portable and can be moved if so desired. So, it's about embracing a simpler lifestyle that's convenient, cosy and creative.

Speaker 2   This is a subject close to Ed's heart! He's even worked on his own tiny home projects.

Speaker 1   That's right! I built the first one myself rather than hiring a construction team. I went that route to cut costs, basically. I was confident I had the skills and expertise. Obviously, if you don't have that knowledge, it might not work out as cost-effective to do so. But I'll own up to making one huge error that I simply hadn't anticipated. You absolutely must check the planning regulations before you start building. I'd assumed I wouldn't need permission for such a small structure. Unfortunately, that wasn't the case, and it was extremely costly to put right.

Interviewer   That's a very important tip, Ed. Christina, are you as fully on board with tiny homes?

Speaker 1   So far, the promotional materials I've seen for tiny homes are still targeting a very narrow market of, dare I say, affluent young professionals. But are tiny homes really suitable for other people? It's not even about the lack of living space. It's more the lifestyle compromises you have to make. Like always planning your meals in advance because there's nowhere to store food, or having very little privacy. And not everyone

Cambridge C2 Proficiency Listening

	is self-sufficient enough to maintain them. But I do understand the appeal of living in a way that reduces consumption and carbon footprints.
Speaker 2	Well, the tiny home sector's still in its infancy. Hopefully Christina's reservations will be resolved as the market grows. For instance, more firms will specialise in building and repairing tiny homes, which will improve the standard and range of options available. It'll also bring the prices down eventually. Personally though, I'd love to see better tiny home infrastructures. Like proper tiny home villages, for instance, to make owners feel less isolated.
Speaker 1	I'm inclined to agree, Ed. People dream of living simply, but they still need access to modern conveniences. Access to a real tiny home community would be ideal. For instance, there could be a central communal kitchen, or a shop selling tiny home supplies.
Interviewer	Thank you both…

Part 4

Audio track: C2_Listening_4_4.mp3

Part 4. You hear five short extracts in which people are talking about their views on literature. For questions 21 to 30, choose from the list A–H.

Extract 1

It takes a certain type of person to love Eda Markham's novels. Someone who finds inappropriate things hilarious, probably! That's why they appeal to me, anyway. The people who dismiss her work are missing out. She doesn't set out to shock just for the sake of causing controversy; she always has a serious message. I wish I'd discovered her work when I was at college. I'd enrolled in a literature class with the intention of delving into new genres. But the syllabus covered the same famous works that high school students are taught. Shouldn't colleges encourage students to discover new things?

Extract 2

Anyone signing up for a literature course obviously has an interest in the subject which they hope will be nurtured. But be ready to have your views challenged, and accept that not everything will match your personal literary interests. The course I took highlighted my ignorance of world literature to the extent that I felt embarrassed when asked to contribute to debates! But I thoroughly enjoyed the experience all the same. As for my personal tastes, I still rate Alan Robinson above other authors. As someone who's spent their entire life in the countryside, the way he conjures up village life in close-knit farming communities is so relatable.

Extract 3

Maybe I wasn't the world's most conscientious pupil as far as homework tasks went, but I always tried to participate in my literature classes. As soon as literature stopped being a compulsory school subject, I dropped it. The novels they made us read were so dull. In fact, I never want to pick up another of the so-called literary 'greats' ever again. For me, good novels are the ones that ask the reader to imagine what they'd do when faced with an impossible situation. That's why I enjoy authors like Mo Yilmaz. His novels deserve far more recognition.

Extract 4

I'm not an avid reader but some novels are what I call 'un-put-down-able'. I use that word when a book's so thrilling that you simply have to finish by reading chapter after chapter. A page-turner, you might say. The best writer for that is unquestionably Daphne Aloisi. She always manages to divert her readers so they never know what's coming next. Her novels generate the most enthusiastic conversations at my book club. For me, talking about a book and hearing other opinions is so satisfying. That comes from an amazing school teacher of mine whose literature classes included the most thought-provoking debates.

Extract 5

Before I enrolled on a literature course last year, I was stuck in a rut with the books I was reading. I hadn't discovered any authors who really resonated with me. I was hoping that taking classes at night school would open up new literary routes to explore. I'm so glad I took the course, because that's how I discovered Jack Kennett. The man's an absolute genius! Nobody else captures the essence of authentic dialogues as well as he does. His stories and themes are wonderful in themselves, but it's the way his characters express themselves that I admire the most.

Cambridge C2 Proficiency Listening

Test 5

Part 1

Audio track: C2_Listening_5_1.mp3

Part 1. You will hear three different extracts. For questions 1 to 6, you must choose the best answer: A, B or C. There are two questions for each extract.

Extract 1 **You hear part of an interview with Ronnie Wilkes, the coach of a professional football club, in which he is asked about an upcoming tournament. Now look at questions 1 and 2.**

Interviewer Ronnie, your team's about to fly out to Dubai for the World Masters Series. But there's been some debate about Harrow Eagles taking part, particularly during such a crucial phase of the domestic season.

Coach Well, it's an honour to compete against teams from all over the world. Commentators are saying it'll take our focus away from the league, but I'm hoping it'll inspire us, if anything. But we also have to be pragmatic. We'll be relying a lot on our youth-team players, which provides a great incentive for them. It's a platform to demonstrate they're ready to make the step up to the first team.

Interviewer Reading between the lines, it sounds as if you're trying to protect your main players. Is physical exhaustion a factor at this stage of the season?

Coach Well, we don't have the biggest squad so it's harder to rest all our players than it is for our rivals. It's difficult to stay fresh when competing in such an intense league. Actually, it's not the physical side of things as much as keeping the mental concentration. There's a wider debate to be had about how many matches we're expected to play, but I'm not sure what the answer is.

Extract 2 **You hear a woman talking to some college students about a marine biology field trip. Now look at questions 3 and 4.**

There are concerns that industrial waste and other pollutants affect not only sea life but also the cleanliness and safety of our beaches. That's why, in collaboration with a partner college, our faculty is investigating the impacts of pollution on the north coast, an area at the heart of our fishing and tourist industries. Our colleagues have already uncovered troubling evidence of unsafe levels of toxic chemicals in the sea. Building on these data, we'll be visiting the research site to investigate marine species. We're particularly concerned about dwindling fish numbers, so we'll be tracking those.

Now, as marine biology postgraduates, the hands-on knowledge you'll gain from conducting research in-situ – I mean in the sea or along the shoreline – is invaluable. In fact, last year, one of our students collected vital data about coastal erosion during a field trip which subsequently formed the basis of her first published paper. So, if you're interested in participating in the research trip, and want to know more about the work you'll be required to do, please contact your tutor. However, I must remind you that any field research comes with certain risks. You won't be permitted to come along unless you attend the safety briefings.

Transcripts

Extract 3   **You hear a man talking on the radio about his work at a bank. Now look at questions 5 and 6.**

When banks invest their customers' money, they rightly have to evaluate the best action to minimise potential losses. But the stereotypical image of banks being risk-averse institutions is outdated. Maybe it's a sign of the growing mistrust of banks. I don't know, but I see it all the time in my role. As a financial planner, I'm there to offer unbiased guidance to account-holders. That's the key thing: not passing judgements about customers' spending habits. But many of the people I meet assume I just want to sell them products and services. And I've spoken to many entrepreneurs with great ideas for start-ups. But it's frustrating that many of them assume my bank will never lend them the capital they need.

But banks aren't necessarily looking for the most professional presentation or the most innovative idea. Whatever your business idea is, I'd like to reassure you that if you can show that you're willing to put in the hard work to make it succeed, then most banks will consider your application. The most impressive applicants that I've seen are the ones who have thought about how their business will develop in the future, and considered possible pitfalls and obstacles. For me, that's vital in business.

Part 2

Audio track: C2_Listening_5_2.mp3

Part 2. You hear a professor of natural history talking about Lark Quarry, a site of scientific interest in Australia. For questions 7 to 15, complete the sentences with a word or short phrase.

Good afternoon, everyone. Today's talk is about the dinosaur tracks, or footprints, discovered at the site called Lark Quarry, located in the Australian state of Queensland.

The ancient dinosaur footprints were found in the 1960s. The person who discovered them, a mining station manager, thought they were the ancient fossilised tracks of birds. It wasn't until palaeontologists excavated the site in the 1970s that a more intriguing scenario was suggested.

The site excavation was a considerable undertaking, involving the removal of some 60 tonnes of rock. In fact, the quarry was named Lark Quarry as a tribute to the hard work of volunteer Malcolm Lark who had the unenviable task of removing most of it. The research team uncovered 3,300 fossilised dinosaur footprints in total.

Clearly, care and precision are crucial when working with ancient fossils. They can be extremely fragile, so ensuring that they come to no harm while studying them can be a very delicate task. Rather than attempting to extract the fossils from the site, copies were taken of the footprints using latex moulds.

The scientists dated the tracks as being approximately ninety-five million years old. Notably, three different types of dinosaur were identified at the site. The first was a *Skartopus australis* theropod, a dinosaur with three toes.

The *Skartopus australis* theropods are the smallest dinosaurs identified at the site, with an average stride length of 62 cm and a footprint size of 4.5 cm. It's assumed that they lived on insects as well as small mammals which they probably hunted in packs.

Moving up in size, there is the 'Winton Foot' dinosaur, named after Winton, a town near Lark Quarry. Unlike the *Skartopous australis*, the 'Winton Foot' dinosaur survived on an entirely plant-based diet. The footprints of this dinosaur show greater variation than those of the *Skartopus australis*. Though the smallest ones are around 4.5cm, larger ones were measured at 30cm.

These two types of dinosaur account for most of the tracks found at Lark Quarry. However, the scientists also detected the presence of a *Tyrannosauropus*, or 'Tyrannosaurus Foot', a nine-metre-tall dinosaur with large, sharp teeth and an average running speed of 30 kilometres an hour. This would undoubtedly have been an intimidating sight for both the *Skartopus australis* and the 'Winton Foot', as they would have been prey for the *Tyrannosauropus*, which was known to have hunted smaller dinosaurs.

In fact, this prompted the research team to posit that the sheer number tracks found at Lark Quarry was evidence of a mass stampede. In other words, the scientists believed the presence of such a dangerous predator meant the other dinosaurs were rushing to flee Lark Quarry. And this has led Lark Quarry to be considered the only known record of a dinosaur stampede.

Visualising a large-scale dinosaur stampede conjures up a dramatic scene, doesn't it? This may be why the iconic stampede scene in the film *Jurassic Park* was reportedly to have been inspired by Lark Quarry. However, this rumour was later debunked as untrue. And while the original interpretations of the Lark Quarry site stimulated great scientific interest in the site, subsequent studies have cast doubt on some of the initial findings.

Nevertheless, Lark Quarry continues to capture the imagination of both scientists and tourists. It's well worth a visit.

Part 3

Audio track: C2_Listening_5_3.mp3

Part 3. You hear a discussion in which academics Gordon Mackie and Sophie Blackmore talk about how communication has changed in society. For questions 16 to 20, choose the best answer: A, B, C or D.

Interviewer — Today we're discussing language, and the role it plays in society. I'm joined by Professor Gordon Mackie and Dr Sophie Blackmore, from Belmont College. Gordon, communication is at the heart of your latest book, isn't it?

Speaker 1 — Exactly so. You only need to watch news reports or read newspaper articles from just a few years ago to see that communication has changed dramatically in the last few decades. And I've obviously devoted a lot of the book to digital communication. We simply cannot ignore how it's transformed the way we express ourselves, and even the slang we use. But the point isn't that these changes are having an adverse impact on language. Not at all. My mission is to show how that view's a myth because, if anything, our language has never been richer.

Speaker 2 — It sounds fascinating! So often in our academic work we deal with the obscure and highly theoretical aspects of linguistics rather than highlight the beauty of everyday communication.

Speaker 1 — Thanks, Sophie. Yes, and what you say about the nature of academic research is particularly true in my field of expertise, historical linguistics. I spend my time exploring how the so-called rules of grammar and spelling have evolved, and the origins of certain taboo expressions. But it's important that I never lose sight of my primary task, which is to gather evidence of the type of language being used at particular times. My role isn't to suggest how language should be, it's to describe how it is, or in my case, how it once was. I preserve documents, not language usage!

Speaker 2 — My role is somewhat different. I do discuss the features that make up effective communication because I teach essay-writing classes. Many university students have a tendency to confuse adopting an appropriate tone with introducing an unnecessarily complex style. Now clearly, university essays should fulfil the conventions of academic writing, and be error-free. However, those things are important only insofar as they help you achieve the key goal, which is to be understood. You may have persuasive arguments, clear evidence, maybe even ground-breaking theories, and that's great. But unless they're expressed in way that is accessible to the reader, your writing cannot be deemed a success.

Transcripts

Speaker 1   And you also research pragmatics, don't you? You've published a lot on the nature of social interaction.

Speaker 2   That's right. Writers choose which information to present, and whether to convey it in an emotional or neutral way. They decide how best to engage the reader. Then, the reader analyses that information and compares it with their existing knowledge. I highlight that point in my classes using the example of social media. When we post something to our network, our followers are already aware of the background. Our intended audience will immediately see the point we're making without us joining all the dots for them. But a stranger might see the same post and interpret it in a completely different way.

Speaker 1   Then there's text language, which has its own particular style and structure. I know it's frowned upon by schools currently, but it'll eventually be studied in the same way that pupils study any other form of writing. After all, it's very inventive. And it's remarkable how universal standards are being adopted within text language. For instance, young people from different cultures can use instant messaging and text language to understand one another without language barriers.

Speaker 2   Yes, it's evolved very quickly. But do you really envisage it appearing on a school syllabus? I can't see any prospect of that. And that's a shame because of course, text language is increasingly accepted by more of the population.

Interviewer   And do you…

Part 4

Audio track: C2_Listening_5_4.mp3

Part 4. You hear five short extracts in which people are talking about their TV-viewing habits. For questions 21 to 30, choose from the list A–H.

Extract 1

My husband and I have quite different views about many issues, so anything about the news or politics is bound to end in an argument. Not that our teenage kids would have any interest in those sorts of programmes, anyway. Sticking to light-hearted shows is a much safer bet because we all share the same sense of humour. That's what we opt for when we're in the mood to watch a bit of TV. And sometimes, there's nothing better than curling up on the sofa with your loved ones, eating chocolate and having a laugh. I really cherish those moments.

Extract 2

These days, the schedules are full of programmes about the quest to discover the nation's best baker, sewing superstar or pottery champion. I find these shows strangely absorbing. Last week, I was watching a painting show, critiquing the artworks and passing judgement on every contestant's performance even though I've never picked up a paintbrush in my life! Seeing the obvious pleasure these pastimes give people has motivated me to try my hand at some of them. I've got back into photography, and even signed up for a beginner's landscape class. But fortunately, my efforts won't be judged by the general public!

Cambridge C2 Proficiency Listening

Extract 3

My family thinks it's hilarious that I tune in regularly to watch soap operas. They don't see the appeal at all. Whenever they watch an episode with me, I end up giving all the backstory. I have to explain who each character's related to or why they bear a particular grudge against another character. I concede that it's not high-quality acting, and the storylines are rather dull. But, bizarrely, that's what I find quite soothing. It's uncomplicated, and I can switch off entirely from my own stresses by watching the ups and downs of fictional families instead!

Extract 4

My sister happily has the TV on in the background without really focusing on the programme, which drives me crazy! When we watch TV together, it's usually for something with a game element. Even if it's just answering questions, we love playing along at home. That's the beauty of these shows. They draw you in by getting you involved, don't they? We don't take them very seriously, but of course we try to beat each other! She's better at science and sport, but I've got the edge when it comes to popular culture.

Extract 5

Because I've got so many other demands on my time, TV isn't a top priority for me these days. I no longer have the patience to watch drama series, to be honest. When I watch something, of course I want it to be presented in an engaging way, but these days I veer more towards informative programmes. The best documentaries for me are the ones that highlight alternative interpretations and all sides of an argument. It's the same with podcasts. I use my commute to work to catch up on my favourite podcasts about everything from crime to sports psychology.

Transcripts

Test 6

Part 1

Audio track: C2_Listening_6_1.mp3

Part 1. You will hear three different extracts. For questions 1 to 6, you must choose the best answer: A, B or C. There are two questions for each extract.

Extract 1 **You hear part of a conversation between two colleagues about a marketing campaign they have developed for a client. Now look at questions 1 and 2.**

Speaker 1 I know it's disheartening when the feedback isn't what you'd been hoping for, but don't get too despondent. There were lots of things the client did approve, like gearing the message towards families.

Speaker 2 I'm just confused about where we went wrong. I'm sure we included everything they specified in the brief. I can't think of what more we could say about the product's design and functionality.

Speaker 1 It's more in the treatment of these selling points. Our advertisement says people's health will be improved using this product. Or implies it at least. From the client's perspective, that's sailing in dangerous waters. Without any official medical evidence, that could open up all sorts of legal implications.

Speaker 2 Will we need to change the concept entirely? That would be a lot of work given the tight deadlines we're working to.

Speaker 1 Well, they've come up with an alternative concept, focusing on how the product brings people together. That's safer territory as far as they're concerned.

Speaker 2 It's not ideal having to change things at this stage, but it's good that they've supplied more guidance. The idea sounds workable, especially if we use the same scenario as before.

Speaker 1 Yes, and ultimately we need to accommodate their wishes.

Extract 2 **You hear a man talking on a podcast about his favourite piece of music. Now look at questions 3 and 4.**

Hearing that gorgeous, dreamy melody and soaring vocal harmonies, I'm immediately transported back to my university days. It's amazing how music can do that! Admittedly, the track I'm referring to, *Slow Fade*, resembles any number of songs from the early nineties. That swirling organ sound was fairly ubiquitous at the time, with lots of bands employing it. But *Slow Fade* stands out because whenever I come back to it, I notice another aspect I hadn't appreciated before. It used to be my favourite party song, but now it's something I listen to when I'm feeling reflective.

Then there are the ambiguous lyrics which leave room for interpretation. My brother and I would argue about them for hours! He was convinced the song's about feeling nostalgic for a long-lost relationship. At the time, I thought the singer was expressing his feeling of isolation, or wanting to connect with people. But I now see it differently. The title hints at something ending. Maybe it's because I'm older now but I've come to see it as the realisation that your time on Earth is limited. So, it's a reminder that you need to live every moment to its fullest. Ultimately, it's a hopeful song.

Cambridge C2 Proficiency Listening

Extract 3 — **You hear a woman talking about a community project being launched in a small fishing village. Now look at questions 5 and 6.**

With its idyllic beaches and picturesque coves, the coastline stretching from Amblewick to Cuttle Bay has seen an influx of visitors in recent years. It's no surprise that local authorities are targeting holidaymakers. In areas where traditional industries such as fishing are in decline, tourism is such a vital source of revenue.

This makes the community project in Polkham so intriguing. Attempting to revitalise the fishing industry is laudable. But how many people would attempt to do so by returning to techniques of the past such as handwoven nets, crab baskets and line fishing?

At its heart this is a project which seeks to remind people of their local heritage and what may soon be lost in the rush to modernise. And, of course, if the venture captures the imagination of visitors to the area, then so much the better.

The vision of bringing Polkham back to its former glory is certainly bold. And the project appears to be off to a good start having attracted the financial backing of a number of prominent families and local businesses. Nevertheless, one wonders whether the project leaders realise quite what they've taken on by attempting such a massive endeavour.

Part 2

Audio track: C2_Listening_6_2.mp3

Part 2. You hear a doctor talking about the health effects of cold water. For questions 7 to 15, complete the sentences with a word or short phrase.

Today's session follows on from the workshop I gave last week on hydrotherapy. To recap, hydrotherapy is a form of treatment which comprises special exercises performed in a shallow pool of warm water.

Now, you may remember from last week's discussion that we talked about how, in hydrotherapy, water temperature is crucial. For instance, research suggests that warm water can aid pain relief while at the same time promoting a sense of relaxation.

But there's also a growing body of evidence pointing towards the therapeutic benefits of cold water, which is what I'm going to discuss today. So, to be clear, I'm going to focus less on the use of cold water to treat patients, and more on its beneficial effects in our everyday lives. We should see it as a simple tool with which we can improve our general wellbeing.

It's important not to overstate what cold water can do. As with any discussion of healthcare, we need to obtain concrete evidence from reputable sources. We must remain dubious when presented with extreme statements claiming cold water is some kind of miracle cure for all ailments.

Nevertheless, the consensus is that regular exposure to cold water can bring some mental, cognitive and physical benefits. One of the ways it can do this is through its effect on the nervous system.

Cold showers induce slight stress on our body as we try to adapt to the cool temperature. So, if we take cold showers regularly, the nervous system eventually gets accustomed to handling moderate levels of stress. This is a process known as 'hardening'. Studies indicate that hardening helps us stay calm when under pressure.

Exposure to cold water also releases certain chemicals in our body, and sends electrical impulses from nerve endings to the brain. Both of these have been found to have a positive effect on the way we feel. In short, these physiological responses are thought to boost our mood, leaving us feeling happy after taking a cold shower.

Cold water may also have a role to play in our cognitive abilities, at least in terms of being alert. Adjusting to cold temperatures stimulates us to inhale and exhale deeply.

Transcripts

These deep breaths lower the levels of CO_2 circulating in the body. Reduced levels of CO_2 have been linked to heightened alertness, enabling us to concentrate for longer intervals.

Physical wellbeing is perhaps the area receiving the greatest attention from the scientific community. Evidence suggests that cold water triggers a change in the way blood is pumped around the body. Blood flows around the body at faster rates when exposed to cold temperatures. This is a natural mechanism that ensure the body maintains its optimal temperature. It's thought increased circulation may help prevent certain cardiovascular conditions.

More generally, cold water may strengthen the body's natural defences against disease. The body protects itself from diseases through the immune system. Research suggests that this system works more efficiently when there are more white blood cells. And crucially, cold temperatures have been shown to result in an increase in white blood cells in the body.

Given all this evidence, the surge in the number of people taking up lake or river swimming is hardly surprising. However, cold showers will suffice if you want to reap the benefits of cold water. And there's no need to make drastic changes to your routine or aim for total immersion in cold water. Instead, gradually build up to this. Start by introducing a short burst of cold water at the end of your shower, and, over time, you'll adapt to longer periods.

Part 3

Audio track: C2_Listening_6_3.mp3

Part 3. You hear part of a discussion in which two business owners, Anya Stern and Vincent Chambers, are talking about their experiences of launching their own businesses. For questions 16 to 20, choose the best answer: A, B, C or D.

Interviewer   Today we're talking about business start-ups. I'm joined by Anya Stern, who set up the Pepper chain of restaurants, and Vincent Chambers, an IT entrepreneur. Anya, where does your entrepreneurial drive come from? Was that encouraged at an early age?

Speaker 1   Well, 'influenced' might be a better word. I passively absorbed useful business insights from my parents. Of course, it was mainly things I'd only appreciate much later. Like the importance of doing things your own way rather than worrying about what other people are doing. But one thing has stuck with me since my childhood. I saw my parents struggling to adapt when e-commerce came in. They put in incredibly long hours to salvage their clothes shop but sadly, it never recovered. It showed me that effort alone isn't enough in business. That sparked my curiosity about why some businesses work and others fail.

Speaker 2   Unlike Anya, I didn't have any business influences in my formative years. Entrepreneurs were just the people I'd seen on TV making million-dollar deals buying and selling things! It didn't dawn on me that there could be IT entrepreneurs, or that I didn't have to fit a specific mould to start my own business. That's why I went down the standard route of working for a large tech giant. Admittedly, it ensured my financial security. And of course, I amassed a lot of invaluable business skills too. But the hardest obstacle was still convincing myself that people like me could run their own business.

Speaker 1   Vincent's point about TV is interesting. There used to be limited opportunities to see business portrayed onscreen. Even now, many programmes purport to be about business, but they're not really. I'm talking about reality competitions where contestants are trying to win investment. I can see how young people might tune in, especially if there are contestants they personally relate to. But the contestants do things they'd never get away with in the real world. Presumably, the content is manipulated by the producers for the sake of entertainment. But how many people with great business ideas are discouraged because of the behaviour they see on

Cambridge C2 Proficiency Listening

these shows? I'd prefer broadcasters to focus on more inspirational business programmes.

Interviewer But what is it that inspires people to want to get into business in the first place?

Speaker 1 One key factor's probably wanting to be your own boss. We all want a say in how things are managed. But it depends on the individual. I've even met people who launched businesses as a hobby after they'd retired and their children had left home. For me, I was desperate to bring Brazilian cuisine to the mass market because I felt the restaurant sector was ready for something new.

Speaker 2 Yes, many entrepreneurs are spurred on by spotting an opportunity. For instance, I wanted to devote my time to virtual reality, which was really compatible with my corporate role. That was my personal tipping point, and I could see potential to transform IT. I hadn't formulated any specific plan at that point, but it felt like it was too important an opportunity to pass up.

Speaker 1 That's exactly the kind of thinking that makes an entrepreneur. Anyone can have a unique business proposition, but not everyone's brave enough to take the plunge, or deal with the negative feedback.

Speaker 2 Yes, because even if your business model isn't particularly innovative, there'll be times when you encounter adversity. So above all, you must be ready to respond to issues as they arise. I'm not saying you should automatically abandon your plans, but be prepared to analyse things logically and without emotion. Then you can deal with whatever comes your way.

Interviewer And I suppose…

Part 4

Audio track: C2_Listening_6_4.mp3

Part 4. You hear five short extracts in which people are talking about decision to pursue postgraduate study – the higher studies some people do after completing their undergraduate degree. For questions 21 to 30, choose from the list A–H.

Extract 1

Postgraduate study is about having your beliefs challenged. If you can reconcile yourself to that, then you'll be amazed at what you can accomplish. During my undergraduate degree, I developed a solid foundation of knowledge, often through set texts that my tutors assigned. That helped me identify my interests, but having to think for myself more during postgraduate studies was a culture shock. There was nobody really telling me exactly what to read or how to interpret the information. I couldn't see the purpose of this at first, but now I really understand the intrinsic value of this, and how far I've come.

Extract 2

In my country, most university students accrue substantial debt during their first degree. So, unless they can get scholarship funding, they either have to enter the workforce immediately to save up for further study, or combine their postgraduate course with part-time work. I opted for the latter. I didn't want to lose momentum by having a long gap before resuming my studies. Postgraduate study has definitely

Transcripts

confirmed that mechanical engineering's the discipline I'm most suited to. But juggling employment with assignments and seminars has been far harder than I'd imagined. Fortunately, my friends are very understanding when I can't see them.

Extract 3

My first degree had a great breadth and variety of modules. That was ideal in terms of keeping my options open. From that perspective, postgraduate study was a very different proposition. Exploring just a few areas in minute detail took quite some adjustment. However, responding to this challenge has cemented what I want to do going forward. I went into postgraduate studies undecided as to whether, at the end of it, I'd go into the corporate world or opt for a career in research. Now that I've nearly completed my master's, I intend to do a doctorate and, eventually, get a teaching position at a university.

Extract 4

My postgraduate studies won't have harmed my career options, I suppose. But if I sound less than enthusiastic, that's because it hasn't been the experience I'd hoped for. Even though I'd saved hard before the course, it's still been a struggle. Reverting to studying after being employed was hard. I really missed having a disposable income. On reflection, it's not been worth it. I've coped well with the workload, but the annoying thing is that studying something so intensively has changed my relationship with the subject. Sadly, I've gone from being fascinated with European history to not wanting to read about it ever again.

Extract 5

Postgraduate study is intellectually stimulating, and I've gained so much support from my professors. A master's course goes beyond simply reading and summarising information. Instead, you should be working towards developing and sharing fresh insights in your discipline. I'd be lying if I said I've found it easy – quite the opposite in fact. I've sometimes questioned whether doing a master's was the right choice because I'm keen to climb the career ladder as quickly as possible. Then again, I wouldn't be able to access the roles I aspire to without a masters, so that makes me feel better.

How to download the audio

To download the accompanying audio files, please visit our website:

prosperityeducation.net/c2-proficiency-audio-download

Use the password TIAB to access this page.

The audio file size for all six tests is approximately 180MB.

Leave us a review

By the way, if you enjoy our book, it would be great if you could leave us a review on Amazon. We're a small publisher and every review makes a difference to us and to our lovely team of authors :-)